Hotfoot to Haworth

MAIN STREET, HAWORTH

Walter White found the climb to the Church was "painfully
steep". This drawing by A Comfort from "A Spring-time
Saunter round and about Bronteland", by Whiteley Turner
(1913), is typical of many Victorian and Edwardian prints.

Hotfoot to Haworth
Pilgrims to the Bronte Shrine

by W R Mitchell

Foreword by Ian Dewhirst
(former Reference Librarian of Keighley)

Various folks are beginning to come boring to Haworth on the wise errand of seeing the scenery described in *Jane Eyre* and *Shirley*...but our rude hills and rugged neighbourhood will I doubt not form a sufficient barrier to the frequent repetition of such visits...

Charlotte Bronte (1850)

CASTLEBERG
1992

A. B. Nicholls

(the husband of Charlotte Bronte)

The Author...

...is the fourth generation of his family to fall under the lure of the Bronte family. He is descended from Dr William Cartman, who preached the sermon in Haworth Church on the Sunday following the funeral of Charlotte Bronte and was a bearer at Patrick Bronte's funeral.

Bill Mitchell, theoretically retired after many years of editing *The Dalesman* and *Cumbria* magazines, continues to devote himself to exploration and research in his beloved North Country.

Castleberg, 18 Yealand Ave., Giggleswick, Settle, North Yorkshire, BD24 0AY

ISBN: 1 871064 75 9

© W R Mitchell, 1992

Typeset in Century Book and printed by J W Lambert & Sons, Station Road, Settle, North Yorkshire, BD24 9AA

Contents

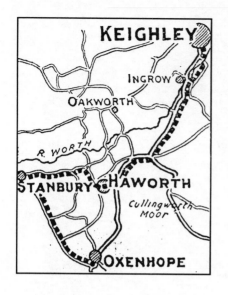

Acknowledgements

To friends in Haworth over a span of 50 years; to the Curators of the Bronte Parsonage Museum since the days when I would pop in for a chat and a cup of tea with Harold Mitchell; and to the Reference staff at Keighley Library, which has its own little Bronte study room.

The Diaeresis

I have had the temerity to drop the diaeresis from the name "Bronte". Writers about the family rue the day when Mr Bronte adopted those two little dots over the letter "e".

Illustrations

Author — 1, 41, 44 (above), 45, 46, 48

The Bronte Society — 4, 43, 44 (bottom)

From "A Spring-time Saunter", by Whiteley Turner — 2, 15, 29

Drawings by T Mackenzie from "Bronte Moors and Villages from Thornton to Haworth", by Elizabeth Southwart (1923) — 30, 96

British Wool Marketing Board — 47.

Foreword by Ian Dewhirst

THERE ARE entire libraries full of books about the Brontes, most of them repetitive, but here Bill Mitchell has contrived a more original approach.

Over and above their works, the Bronte's lives and landscape have always caught the popular imagination. Probably only a well-read devotee of Jane Austen or George Eliot could tell you anything about how or where they lived, but the general public—without necessarily having read an actual Bronte page—seems readily informed on a Haworth and its surroundings invariably described as bleak.

The popular conception, now largely nurtured on radio and television, is not strictly accurate. A television series with which I was once involved exuberantly voiced a "casting-off of the whalebone and running free on the moors" view of the Bronte girls. I was allowed to suggest the more staid reality of an early Victorian clergyman's daughters in a landscape rather busy with quarries, farms and coal pits; but the "running free" impression predominated. The moors have indeed depopulated since the Brontes' day, but this is a difficult idea for the average Bronte fan to come to terms with.

Not that earlier Bronte topographers are blameless. To them we stand indebted for a whole mythology of association, whereby a commonplace farmstead at Top Withens became the model for a Wuthering Heights to which it bears not the slightest resemblance; whilst the destination of Charlotte's last walk and fatal cold was confidently fixed upon as the insipid "Bronte Waterfall". In fact, some of the first-generation Bronte commentators located the latter at Ponden Kirk (colloquially known in the 1880s as "Wuthering Heights"), but the "Bronte Waterfall", being more accessible to the literary sightseer, prevailed.

Bill Mitchell, in tracing a development from first pilgrims to mass tourism, helps us to see the Bronte phenomenon in a new context.

We agree that too much has been written about the Brontes, far too much has been surmised. More than any other writer they have been the prey of the sentimental hero-worshipper and sensation-monger.

While they have been shamelessly commercialized, their work has been over-estimated.

It is with a smile rather supercilious that we take up again the books that they have written, and the books that have been written about them. We close the last one—and find that the madness has entered our own blood.

Elizabeth Southwart (1923).

We perceived as we passed the post-office, that visitors were now expected at Haworth, for in the little window were copies of Charlotte Bronte's works; those of her sisters; Mrs Gaskell's *Life of Charlotte Bronte;* also photographs of the Rev Mr Bronte and of the church and parsonage.

W H Cook (1868).

I cannot help feeling at times a grain of pity for those unfortunate ladies who hired a Bronte for service in their schoolrooms. Always trailing their threadbare but neatly-darned cloaks in quest of real or fancied insults, out of sympathy with their charges, devoid or almost devoid of the saving grace of humour, and filled with a nostalgic desire for their own home, they must surely have been a severe trial to their employers.

Lady Wilson, of Eshton Hall.

Obsession, vendetta, bigamy, insanity and illicit love. Surely not the writings of the shy spinster daughters of a country parson?

"South Pennine", issued for tourists (1991).

Introduction

The Japanese find *Wuthering Heights* charming. We don't
understand its charm, but trying to fathom it is delightful.
Prof. Hiroshi Nakaoka (1976).

HAWORTH without the Brontes would be just another gritstone
village on the Southern Pennines. Now it is a destination in itself.
Haworth has become a Bronte theme park. So many Japanese visitors
are being recorded that moorland signposts have been provided with
Japanese sub-titles, the expense having been met by the Countryside
Commission.

The Parsonage is the second most popular literary shrine in the
land, visited by pilgrims who have been emotionally moved by the
strange, sad lives of Patrick and Maria Bronte and their six children,
all of whom, save the head of the household, died young.

Genius flowered briefly in this unpromising moor-edge setting. Enduring works of literature were penned in a large but compact
Georgian house overlooking mossy ranks of gravestones and the
parish church. Celtic imaginations were stirred by the wind-ruffled
moors where mutton and wool from innumerable sheep provided a
basis living for small-time farmers who moved about the scene, crooks
in hand, dogs at heel, like minor characters from a Victorian
melodrama.

The Bronte children, imaginative offspring of an Irish father and
Cornish mother, shared the parish of Haworth with some 4,000 other
people; the children also had private worlds of their own—Glasstown,
Angria and Gondal—created in the recesses of the Parsonage during
play, to be chronicled in tiny notebooks, using miniscule script.

Becoming increasingly sophisticated with the passing years, such
literary activity led directly to the writing of novels. And what
novels! The Brontes penned some of the finest ever written in
English.

The Bronte years at Haworth (1820-1861) coincided with a period of momentous social change. The clack of thousands of domestic hand-looms was giving way to the clatter of power looms. The Brontes, trudging down the hill to Keighley, saw striking evidence of the new milldom in the palatial factories and a mini-forest of smoking chimneys.

It took many years to eradicate the urban squalor of open drains, primitive toilets and other unhygenic features of life that led to a high infant mortality and, for many of the survivors, to a succession of chronic illnesses. The weakly Bronte children, looking from the Parsonage windows on to battalions of tombstones, had a daily reminder of the fleeting nature of human life.

The Bronte Moors, celebrated especially through Emily Bronte's powerful novel, *Wuthering Heights,* formed just one of many tracts of sour, heathery ground on the Southern Pennines. This was not quite the wilderness the visitor expected, having read the book. The reek of peat fires flavoured the moorland air, for there was a scattering of farms, no less than three of which were named Withens. It was subsistence farming, the income augmented by whatever the children could earn in the new-fangled mills.

The four decades of the Bronte occupation of Haworth Parsonage represent but a blink in the history of this moor-edge settlement. Haworth, in the old contemplative days, was a place for poets and preachers, of whom William Grimshaw—cleric and friend of the Wesley brothers—was widely renowned for his physical and spiritual zest. He routed the forces of evil.

Forty years is long only in terms of the human life-span. Yet the Bronte way of life has become part of English folk-lore. A memorial tablet in Haworth Church, marking the last resting place of all the family, save Anne (who was buried in Scarborough) provides the necessary focal point for literary pilgrims.

The old Haworth Parsonage is a museum, the exhibits including Charlotte's wedding dress, indicating by its size how slight of build she was and drawing from a local visitor the comment: "I reckon there'd be more flesh on a walking stick".

The Bronte cult began quietly, when a leisured and literate few, having read the novels, and hearing of the deaths of all the Brontes save Charlotte, came to Haworth in the hope of observing the celebrated authoress. A visitor slipping into church on a Sunday might actually see Charlotte at her devotions and her father preaching from the top deck of the three-decker pulpit. A few fans had the temerity to visit the Parsonage.

The Bronte cult had an indeterminate start. In 1866, a visitor who subsequently wrote in the *Mercury Supplement* (Leeds) described the village as "gloomy and unprepossessing" and could find little interest among the local people in "the wonderful story of the parson's daughters".

Mrs. Gaskell, in *The Life of Charlotte Bronte,* which was written at the behest of Patrick Bronte and published while he was still alive, gave Brontephiles something akin to a sacred text. The author was to be described as a legend-monger. The cult was sustained by fulsome articles in the newspapers and books by admirers. During this century, the Brontes have featured on radio, television and cinema films, in which the "wuthering" wind is ceaselessly heard.

In France, Charlotte had literary acclaim not long after her great talent had been recognised in England. Russia soon had its Bronte fans and a Russian edition of a Bronte work was published in St Petersburg as early as 1903. The Japanese are a nation of Bronte admirers, with Emily's great novel as a firm favourite. It has been estimated that 100,000 Japanese pilgrims a year attend the Bronte shrine.

From the earliest days, the fictional people and places became firmly associated with local characters and situations. The covers of many books show the remains of Top Withens with the implication that this shorn-off and cemented remnant of an old farmstead inspired the setting for *Wuthering Heights.*

On many books, Branwell Bronte's famous painting of his three sisters appears by courtesy of the National Portrait Gallery. Another favourite subject is Patrick Bronte, with his wire-framed spectacles and high neck collar.

We know a great deal, but the Brontes still elude us, hence the proliferation of theories about their lives and work. They remain an enigma. No one has yet caught and displayed them like butterflies in a collection. And everyone loves a mystery.

The Bronte Connection attracts about 200,000 paying visitors a year to the Parsonage. Many more shuffle through Haworth Church, though this is not the one known to the Brontes. Their church, with its three-decker pulpit, from which that "hell-fire" preacher, William Grimshaw, admonished his flock, was replaced in post-Bronte days by a Victorian Gothic structure of the type that had become popular throughout the land.

"People just love to come to Haworth for a day out," said a local woman who found the gala atmosphere of summer quite stimulating. For the first fans, the experience could be awesome. John Stores Smith, a Mancunian visiting Haworth in 1850, was conducted into the parlour at the Parsonage. Miss Bronte was "standing in the full light of the window, and I had ample opportunity of fixing her upon my memory, where her image is vividly present to this hour..."

The author of *Jane Eyre* was "diminutive in height, and extremely fragile in figure. Her hand was one of the smallest I have ever grasped... Her complexion had no trace of colour in it, and her lips were pallid also; but she had a most sweet smile, with a touch of tender melancholy in it."

I am the fourth generation of my family to have been moved by the Brontes, their sad lives and their strange but compelling prose and verse. A maternal ancestor, Dr Cartman, of Bingley, was a personal friend of the Rev Patrick Bronte who sometimes stayed at the Parsonage and once delighted his old friend by giving him an early form of crampon—a device to be fitted to the feet which would enable him to walk safely on snow or ice.

It was Dr Cartman who preached in Haworth Church on the Sunday following Charlotte's funeral. He was one of the clerics who carried the coffin in which Patrick reposed to his last resting place.

My paternal grandfather's bookshelf held copies of all the Bronte novels and he occasionally sent off an article to a local newspaper about the family, concentrating (quite rightly) on the religious aspects of their lives, which many modern writers play down, and interspersing his text with verses taken from the (somewhat sad) Bronte hymns.

Father and I were among the comparatively few pilgrims who chose to make an off-season journey to Haworth. In November murk and drizzle, which enhanced the Bronte sadness and brought a gleam to the mosses and lichen in the mini-forest of tombstones, I saw the Parsonage rising beyond the churchyard wall.

In the 1950s, when I followed the family tradition of scribblemania and produced a booklet about the Brontes, no more than 50,000 visitors a year were paying for admission to the Parsonage and local tradesfolk had a few specific Bronte wares. The word "hype" was still only a wrestling term.

The first Bronte fans faced a weary slog from Keighley, for the Worth Valley railway did not exist. In due course they reached Haworth, which appears to have been stuck on a damp hillside. A languid summer day was suited to Bronte viewing but in January, 1867, W H Cooke and "a literary friend" braved a countryside lying a foot deep in snow.

Wrote Mr Cooke: "The people whom we pass on the road stare hard at us, as though strangers were a rarity in this part. Each passer-by, we notice, instead of shoes or boots, wears wooden clogs, which clank noisily as he proceeds on his way. The sky overhead looked heavy and threatening; whilst in every direction, far as the eye could reach, were hills upon hills of sullen outline..."

Haworth seemed to the wanderers to be situated amongst the clouds, "for the village stands on the side of a steep hill which is crowned...by the village church.

From the very back of the church rise the wild moors—the clouds and moors seeming in truth almost to merge themselves in one at the back of the sacred edifice".

It seemed to me, while visiting Haworth by bus in the days before the demolition man thinned out the high density housing beside the road from Keighley, as though the architecture fell into a definite pattern—mill, row of dark terraced houses, Co-operative stores, chapel. This pattern was varied here and there by advertisement hoardings dealing with such un-Bronteish subjects as fruit drinks and detergents. You could tell the chapels from the mills because the former had arched windows.

Mill, terrace, stores, chapel—so it went on until I was in sight of that ragged cluster of buildings on the Pennine skyline which was old Haworth, linked to its newer half by a steep slope. I would hesitate at the edge of the setts, which most writers wrongly describe as "cobbles". It was impressive to see how the dressed blocks held together on such a gradient. I had a feeling that if I had removed half a dozen the whole lot would shutter down.

Another time, when driving a car, my teeth rattled like castanets throughout the full length of the steep street, which is now out of bounds to motorists, except for access, and has been ruined at the bottom end by the demolition of the tiny yards which gave it a sense of mystery.

I first knew Haworth when tales about the Brontes, passed down from parents or grandparents, featured in every local interview. Fred Toothill's grandfather, Jack, was the village barber who counted Patrick Bronte among his customers and charged him three farthings for a shave.

Jack, asked about the Brontes, invariably replied: "Nay, lad, nobody bothered with 'em. They were snobs".

Patrick called at the shop just as another customer was using bad language. The parson suggested that he might read the Good Book. The swearer said he had a more important book—his Rent Book. Mr Bronte is said to have given him half-a-crown towards the rent.

A descendant of Jack Toothill told me of one of the barber's favourite Bronte tales, which had "come down in the family". A visitor to the Parsonage, seeing some oatcakes hanging to dry from the overhead rack known as a "bread-fleak" thought he was seeing rows of wash-leathers.

Haworth folk have not made a fuss about the Brontes while having a quiet pride in a family whose presence ensures that their village is famous the world over. One old chap delivered milk to the back door of the Parsonage for years before he could be persuaded to look round. He recognised many of the objects. He had known Mr Bronte!

Almost all the authors have been "off-comers". One of my favourites is *The Bronte Story,* written by Margaret Lane and delightfully illustrated in scraperboard by Joan Hassall. Author and artist met when Margaret Lane was well advanced with the book, and so many pictures were required that Joan Hassall had to resort to scraperboard drawings, which could be completed more quickly than the engravings she would have preferred.

"We went up to Haworth together," Joan told me. "I remember

that the boarding accommodation we found was rather small and chilly. There was not really a sitting room, so we used to go to bed very early. Margaret got into bed and I sat in an old wicker chair and was well wrapped up. Then we went through the typescript, deciding what would be good to illustrate.''

Margaret Lane had a car and they would drive about the district. Joan Hassall made sketches. She was fortunate in being loaned some old photographs, so the illustrations for the book were "a mixture of my sketches and old photographs''.

On my own visits to the Parsonage, I enjoyed a natter over a cup of tea with Harold G Mitchell, who had been the curator since the Parsonage Museum was opened in 1928. When talk turned to the Bronte cult, he considered that the many tragedies in the Bronte lives were the main reason for the interest.

Harold spent an hour showing two old ladies round the Parsonage. As he bade farewell to them on the doorstep, one asked: "Who did you say lived here?''

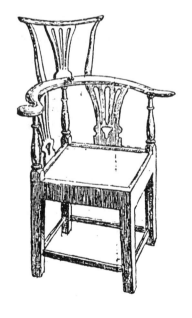

Two "Bronte relics''.
Left — Branwell Bronte's "corner chair'' from the Black Bull at Haworth.
Right — A toy iron which had belonged to Charlotte Bronte.

15

1. Now Read On...
The Bronte Story in Brief

Their story is the most romantic in the history of literature, full
of comedy and pathos, yet bearing witness to the indomitable spirit
that dwelt within these weakly consumptive girls.
C E M Joad (The New Leader, 1924).

THE BRONTE girls—Charlotte, Emily and Anne—were the offspring
of parents who had a Celtic background, so it was inevitable that their
writing would be strong and imaginative.

Their father, Patrick Bronte (1777-1861), was a poor Irish boy who
made good. His surname was Brunty and he hailed from Emdale near
Loughbrickland, in County Down. His father, Hugh, illiterate and
penniless, was a Protestant who provided his Catholic wife with a
two-roomed, mud-floored and thatched cottage and 10 children, of
whom Patrick was the eldest, being so named because he was born on
St Patrick's Day.

Mrs Brunty renounced her faith. The children were raised as Pro-
testants. Patrick taught himself to read, using his father's Bible and
works by Bunyan and Burns. Patrick's good fortune was to have his
keen and intelligent manner noticed by a Presbyterian clergyman,
who helped him up the lower rungs of the social ladder, leading to his
appointment at a Church school, followed by a position as tutor to the
sons of a Rector who, to Patrick's joy, had a fine library.

The poor Irish lad gained admission to St John's College, Cambridge,
where, on October 1, 1802, his name was recorded as "Patrick
Branty". He shortly afterwards changed his name to Bronte, after
Lord Nelson, his great hero, who in 1799 was created Duke of Bronte.

Patrick's years of study led him to Cambridge, to a BA degree and
to his ordination and curacies in Essex, Shropshire and the West
Riding. In 1811, when still a bachelor, he became minister of
Hartshead-cum-Clifton.

Mrs Gaskell, in her biography of Charlotte, was to describe him as being a "very handsome fellow, full of Irish enthusiasm, and with something of an Irishman's capacity of falling easily in love".

His single state ended when he met Maria Branwell, an attractive Cornish woman some 30 years of age, at the home of her uncle, John Fennell, master of Woodhouse Grove School. Maria's parents had died but she had a good annuity on which to live. It was a brief, happy courtship in which Maria referred to her young man as her dear "saucy Pat". They were married at Guiseley Church, on December 29, 1812.

Maria Bronte bore him six children, Maria and Elizabeth being born at Hartshead, the others at Thornton, near Bradford, to which place the family moved in 1815. Patrick was to recall: "My happiest days were spent there. . . ." The family "flitted" to Haworth in April, 1820. Patrick, appointed Perpetual Curate with a stipend of £200, had the spiritual oversight of over 4,000 people living in the merest part of a parish of over 10,000 acres. Most of it consisted of open moorland.

Maria Branwell collapsed with terminal cancer in January 1821. She died in the following September, her last words being: "Oh, my poor children!" Patrick, the widower, did make some efforts to marry for a second time, but then lapsed into grey widowerhood, a state which lasted for some 40 years.

The children were subsequently cared for by Miss Elizabeth Branwell (1776-1842) who, as Maria's elder sister, was known respectfully as Aunt Branwell and is recalled as "a small antiquated lady". She was none too thrilled by damp and dirty Haworth or by the moors with their "wuthering" wind. She also had a particularly gloomy brand of Calvinistic religion. Yet the children grew up in a cheerful place, inhabited by people and several household pets.

The village, like others, might be squalid by modern standards of hygiene; the funeral bell was tolled far too often, but the clouds were not always "mucky" and often the west wind swept them away to reveal all with clarity and colour.

It was a narrow, even restricting life, much of it spent within four walls. If they could not fully share in the affairs of the big world, they could create worlds of their own, and this they did, developing a fantasy life based on mini-kingdoms—prompted, in the first place, by gifts bought in Leeds by their father, a box of wooden soldiers for Branwell—Mr Bronte was excited by military history—and a model village, among other things, for the girls.

The stories they devised around the soldiers and other objects tapped their springs of imagination and released creative energy that led in stages to the novels for which they became famous.

Patrick, curate at Haworth, had a strong social conscience and a desire to help the more deprived of his parishioners.

Charlotte, in her little "History of the Year 1829" gives the flavour of Parsonage life when things were going well: "Tabby, the servant, is washing up the breakfast-things, and Anne, my youngest sister...is kneeling on a chair, looking at some cakes which Tabby has been baking for us...Aunt is upstairs in her room, and I am sitting by the table writing this in the kitchen".

The family troubles, which had begun with the death of Mrs Bronte, continued in 1824 when the children were sent to the newly-opened Clergy Daughters' School at Cowan Bridge, an institution presided over by William Carus Wilson, clergyman and landowner. They arrived in summer and had to withstand a grim winter. In the spring, an outbreak of "low fever" occurred and in their already weakened state the two youngest sisters were brought back to Haworth, here to die from consumption. Charlotte, with few happy memories of the place, used Carus Wilson—somewhat unfairly—as the model for Mr Brocklehurst in *Jane Eyre*.

It was the end of formal schooling for the remaining children—Charlotte, Branwell, Emily and Anne. Thrown back on themselves and their imagination, they continued to develop a fantasy world, recording its affairs—as already noted—in tiny books.

An enlightened father encouraged the awakening of their minds by making his excellent library available. The Bronte children were impressed by the somewhat radical pulpit oratory of the time. They soaked into their consciousness the local tales which they heard in Haworth or were related to them by the Bronte servants.

They were nonetheless ill-equipped to take up adult employment. For the parson's daughters, who must have respectable work, there was little else to do but become teachers in private schools or governesses to the (usually pampered) offspring of people with means.

The Brontes went forth to work for various well-to-do families and returned home miserable and homesick. Their brilliant brother, Branwell, found employment of a kind but dissipated his talents, descending into alcoholism, drug addition and an early death.

The three surviving girls, deciding to have their own school, and needing to be more proficient at languages, Charlotte and Emily completed their education at a school run in Brussels by the Hegers.

Miss Branwell died (painfully) in October, 1842, and the sisters returned home, Emily to stay but Charlotte to return to Brussels as a student teacher, at the suggestion of M Heger, whose brilliant mind she admired.

Not only had the Brontes a home in Yorkshire; there was pure "Yorksher" in that place through the ministrations and dialect-laden speech of two faithful servants who were also friends of the family. Their names were Tabitha and Martha. They had a great fund of local stories which, doubtless, coloured the writings and the dreams of the growing Bronte girls. Tabitha had known people who, when walking by the beck on a moonlit night, had seen fairies at play!

Tabitha began work at the Parsonage when Charlotte was some nine years of age; she stayed for 30 years and her death preceded that of Charlotte by just a few months. The younger servant, Martha, was the daughter of John Brown, sexton, grave-digger and special friend of Branwell Bronte.

At the Parsonage at Haworth, the girls, using the pseudonyms of Currer, Ellis and Acton Bell, wrote a book of poems which was published in 1846. Two copies were sold. Literary success came in 1847, with the publication of Charlotte's novel *Jane Eyre*, followed by Emily's *Wuthering Heights* and Anne's *Agnes Grey*. Again, they used pen-names.

It was a heady time for the three sisters. Into the Parsonage came periodicals and newspapers with reviews of their work. Emily's genius was concealed by the name Ellis Bell. It is to the credit of many reviewers that they not only read *Wuthering Heights,* which appeared amid a welter of prim Victorian novels, but more than a few literary critics acknowledged that the Bronte talent was out of the ordinary. It was presumed at first that the authors were men.

Wuthering Heights was (and is) a strange book. The somewhat prim review of the *Examiner,* in a review published on January 8, 1848, wrote of Heathcliff as "an incarnation of evil qualities; implacable hate, ingratitude, cruelty, falsehood, selfishness, and revenge... and it is with difficulty that we can prevail upon ourself to believe in the appearance of such a phenomenon, so near our own dwellings as the summit of a Lancashire or Yorkshire moor".

The Bronte story had a down-turn with the deaths of brother and two sisters—Branwell, Emily and Anne. The old parson and Charlotte lived on at the Parsonage. For Charlotte, a moment of happiness, if not true love, came with her brief marriage to the Rev Arthur Bell Nicholls, her father's curate.

Mr Bronte had objected to the match, fearing for the health of his one remaining daughter. Despite her weak constitution, Charlotte became pregnant. Then, going for a moorland walk with her husband in wild weather she picked up a chill. Charlotte took to her bed and, ere long, she was dead.

Bronte, though old and weary, preached in Haworth church until he lacked the physical energy to climb the pulpit steps. One who heard him recorded that his text was from Job iii. 17: "There the wicked cease from troubling; and there the weary be at rest." He talked extemporaneously, "without effort, in short, easy sentences,—and was drawn, it appeared to me, right out of that old graveyard, among whose stones his feet had walked, and his imagination had lived so long".

Mr Nicholls and Martha Brown remained with the old man at the Parsonage until his death, aged 84, in June, 1861. Mr Nicholls, released from his Haworth responsibilities, went off to Ireland, took up farming, married a cousin and died peacefully in 1906.

2. Hotfoot to Haworth
The First Fans Appear

Mills and scattered cottages chase romance from these valleys.
Charlotte Bronte.

...and there, just beyond the crowded graves, stands the parsonage, as unsmiling as the church.
Walter White, a visitor when Mr Bronte was still alive.

DURING the last five years of Charlotte's life, and the last 10 years of the life of her father, strangers arrived at Haworth and inquired about the Bronte novels—the writers and the settings.

The Bronte servants were soon quizzing Charlotte about "Currer Bell" and at first her replies were devious. Charlotte's book *Shirley*, being something of a documentary of the early days of industrialisation, was sprinkled with references to actual places, which stimulated tourism.

Charlotte was a familiar figure to the Haworthians and, with luck, a visitor might see her neat and tiny figure moving about the village, calling on some of the old ladies or sitting in the parson's pew at church.

Those who were not lucky arrived when Charlotte was on her travels—off to Gawthorpe Hall, at Padiham, or Briery Close, Windermere, to spend a few days in the company of Sir James Kay-Shuttleworth and his wife or down to London for a meeting with George Smith, her publisher. She might even be a guest of the Gaskells in Manchester.

In the springtime of 1852 she took herself off to the Yorkshire coast, staying at Filey and visiting Scarborough, to see the grave of her sister Anne.

At first, when there was a guessing game about the celebrated author Currer Bell, her presence did not create a stir. Then, as she wrote to W S Williams, of her publishers, Smith Elder, in November, 1849:

"During my late visit I have too often had reason, sometimes in a pleasant, sometimes in a painful form, to fear that I no longer walk invisible. *Jane Eyre,* it appears, has been read all over the district—a fact of which I never dreamt—I met sometimes with new deference, with augmented kindness: old schoolfellows and old teachers, too, greeted me with generous warmth. And, again, ecclesiastical brows lowered thunder at me".

On the publication of *Jane Eyre,* the *Christian Remembrancer* for April 1848, noted: "The name and sex of the writer are still a mystery...However, we, for our part, cannot doubt that the book is written by a female, and, as certain provincialisms indicate, by one from the North of England".

Jane Eyre impressed by being something different from the run-of-the-mill romances of the time—a strange tale of a Plain Jane's harsh upbringing, her employment as a governess (what else, knowing Charlotte?) at Thornfield Hall by Edward Rochester, the riddle of a locked room from which mirthless laughter is heard, misunderstanding, intrigue, love, escape from a bigamous marriage to Rochester, flight, return, reconciliation and—"Reader, I married him."

Then there was that complex novel, *Shirley,* with a large cast set against the dramatic, sometimes violent social movements of the time. Mr Bronte had given his children first-hand accounts of the arrival of the power looms. He had encouraged them to read about the real world in contemporary newspapers.

Charlotte, ever a stylish writer, noted in *Shirley:* "Of late years, I say, an abundant shower of curates has fallen upon the north of England: but in eighteen-hundred-eleven-twelve that affluent rain had not descended: curates were scarce then: there was no Pastoral Aid—no Additional Curate's Society to stretch a helping hand to worn-out rectors and incumbents, and give them the wherewithal to pay a vigorous young colleage from Oxford or Cambridge..."

The sales of *Shirley* initially suffered from a comparison with *Jane Eyre. The Times,* December 7, 1849, ended its note with the words "millions understood her before—she may count by units those who will appreciate her now". Not for the first time, *The Times* was wrong. It was *Shirley,* with its realism, rather than Jane Eyre, that stimulated the first literary pilgrimages to Haworth.

Charlotte was still alive, married to Mr Nicholls. There was nothing of the literary romance about this marriage. Charlotte wrote to Ellen Nussey in April, 1854: "What I taste of happiness is of the soberist order. I trust to love my husband—I am grateful for his tender love to me".

Visitors who knocked on the door of the parsonage or who got the sexton to present their cards were ushered into the parlour by Martha Brown or maybe Charlotte herself. If Mr Bronte was in a good mood, he consented to see the fans.

The Duke of Devonshire arrived with a brace of grouse. From many parts of the world came requests for specimens of Charlotte's handwriting, which the obliging Patrick Bronte met by cutting up and distributing some of the letters his daughter had written.

It was in these later times that my ancestor, William Cartman, came into the Bronte picture.

Cartman, a native of Ripon, lived at Bingley from 1818, being usher of the Grammar School and then a curate of Bingley Parish Church. He subsequently moved to Skipton as curate at the Parish Church and, from 1841 until 1867, as headmaster of Ermysted's Grammar School.

Charlotte, now a celebrity under her own name, was earning an estimated £1,500 a year through her literary activities. Visiting London and then spending three days with Mrs Gaskell in Manchester before returning to Haworth, she wrote to her father ("Dear Papa") expressing pleasure that he was in pretty good health and that "Mr Cartman came to help you on Sunday".

The decorators had arrived at the parsonage. "I fear you will not have had a very comfortable week in the dining-room; but by this time I suppose the parlour reformation will be nearly completed, and you will soon be able to return to your old quarters".

Three days after the funeral of Charlotte Bronte, Cartman arrived from Skipton to stay the night at Haworth Parsonage. On the following morning, Sunday, April 8, he conducted the funeral service. Patrick sat erect and attentive as the good doctor preached from the text: "And all wept, and bewailed her: but he said. Weep not; she is not dead, but sleepeth" (Luke 8, v52).

At 82, almost blind, sitting alone in his room at the Parsonage, perhaps brooding on the deaths of members of his large family, Patrick could still show compassion towards others. A villager had just lost a two-year-old daughter, a victim of scarlet fever. Patrick wrote her a letter of consolation.

Stacey Marks, RA, who decorated two or three churches in the neighbourhood of Halifax, made the pilgrimage to Haworth with a friend. They heard Mr Bronte preach from the top deck of the pulpit, while at the reading-desk below sat Mr Nicholls. The two artists, admitted to the Parsonage after the service, were treated genially and left with a few flowers "as a remembrance of the gifted sisters".

Tyndall, a railway surveyor engaged in field work for the proposed Worth Valley Railway completed his work at nightfall on a wild day. When he was barely able to read the figures on his levelling staff, "I placed my last 'bench mark' on a tombstone in Haworth Churchyard. Close at hand was the vicarage of Mr Bronte, where the genius was nursed that soon afterwards burst forth and astonished the world".

Walter White, a Londoner, author of *A Month in Yorkshire,* undertook the "painfully steep" climb up Main Street, remarking: "What a wearisome hill; you will half doubt whether horses can draw a load up it".

White saw the usual signs of an awakening tourist age, noting: "Some of the windows denote an expectation of visitors; the apothecary exhibits photographs of the church, the parsonage and Mr Bronte; and no one seems surprised at your arrival".

While breakfasting at the *Black Bull,* he listened to the chitter-chatter of the hostess about the Brontes. "Mr Nicholls had preached the day before in the morning; Mr Bronte in the afternoon. It was mostly in the afternoon that the old gentleman preached, and he delivered his sermon without a book. The people felt sorry for his bereavements; and they all liked Mr Nicholls".

The sexton admitted White to the church. "He points to the low roof, and quotes Milton, and leads you to the family pew, and shows you the corner where she—that is, Charlotte—used to sit; and against the wall, but a few feet from this corner, you see the long plain memorial stone, with its melancholy list of names.

"As they descend, the inscriptions crowd close together; and beneath the lowest, that which records the decease of her who wrote *Jane Eyre*, there remains but a narrow blank for those which are to follow..."

In the vestry, the sexton displayed the marriage register with the signatures of Charlotte Bronte, her husband and father; and next, his collection of photographs, any of which could be purchased. "When he saw that I had not the slightest inclination to become a purchaser, to have seen the place was quite enough; he said, that if I had a card to send in, the old gentleman would see me. It seemed to me, I replied, that the greatest kindness a stranger could show to his venerable pastor, would be, not to intrude upon him".

Professor John Elliot Cairnes, of Trinity College, Dublin, climbed the Main Street in September 1858 only to hear that he had just missed an opportunity to hear Patrick Bronte preach. The garrulous sexton told him about it, explaining that sometimes the cleric suffered from "attacks of illness".

Cairnes sought out the memorial tablet, described by Mrs Gaskell. He was shown the parsonage pew and then, deciding to pay his respects to the old gentleman at the Parsonage, he sent in his card. "I was informed that Mr Bronte had, a few hours previously, retired to bed, not feeling well, but that he hoped I wd walk in & see the house. This I, of course, did under the guidance of the maid, Martha (mentioned by Mrs Gaskell)".

He was to remember Martha's dark eyes and hair; she was an interesting girl who would have been pretty but for the loss of nearly all her front teeth.

W H Cooke, calling at the church in January, 1867, heard from the loquacious sexton (the son of the sexton who had been a great friend of Branwell Bronte) that the Brontes did little visiting about the village; "they were fonder of taking long walks by themselves on the moors. Many a time, sir, have I seen them, along with their dogs, going up that path...

"Yes, Emily was very reserved. Anne was the loveliest, sir. Whenever they were baking at the parsonage, she always took care to make me—I was a little lad, then, you know, sir—an apple pasty; or, if she couldn't make me one, then she would give me a handful of raisins, or something of that sort. . ."

Branwell? "Oh, yes, I knew him well, too". He was clever, was Mr Branwell. "I have seen him take two quills, one in each hand, and write two letters at once on two different subjects, whilst some one kept talking with him. He wrote just as easily with the left hand as with the right. The way he first began to write with both hands, he told me, was this. One day he was at a railway station, and he wanted very much to get two letters written before the train came up, and it occurred to him that he might as well write them both at once. He tried, and found he could do it quite well".

Mr Nicholls? "A nice man he was. Quiet, you know, but very kind, and a real good hard-worker".

Mrs Gaskell? ". . . we don't like her nor yet her book. She says something about us folk that isn't true".

James M Hoppin, from America (1867) was shown by Martha into Patrick Bronte's study. "Mr Bronte met me with real kindness of manner, but with something of the stateliness of the old school. His hair, worn short, was white as driven snow; his ample cambric cravat completely covered his chin; and his black dress was of the most scrupulous neatness.

"He has been called handsome, but that he never could have been. He has strong, rugged, even harsh features, with a high, wrinkled forehead, and swarthy complexion; and his eyes are partially closed, for he is almost blind. . .

"Our conversation was chiefly on religious topics, and he wished to be informed about the great spiritual movements which from time to time pass over America. He thought that revivals in England and Ireland were accompanied by too much animal excitement; yet he believed in their reality. . .

"He struck me as being naturally a very social man, with a mind fond of discussion, and feeding eagerly on new ideas, in spite of his reserve. . ."

Hoppin heard the old man preach from a text in Job (iii. 17). "In parts it was pathetic, especially where he alluded to the loss of children. He branched off upon the sorrows, convulsions, and troubles then in the world, and he seemed to long for wings like a dove to fly away from this changeful scene, and be at rest. The old church clock, as if echoing the venerable preacher's remarks, had written upon it, 'Time how short—eternity how long!'."

In the summer of 1860, Patrick (Parson Pat) preached his last sermon. By autumn, he was virtually confined to his bed. It was left to Mr Nicholls to run the parish; he was kindly but straight-laced and objected when the parents of children to be christened wanted to name them after the Bronte sisters. Patrick, flattered by the idea, conducted bedroom baptisms. Into his room were smuggled registers, parents and children. He baptised them while propped up in bed, using water from a jug.

Patrick died on June 7, 1861, aged 84. His body was borne into Haworth Church five days later. *The Bradford Review* noted: "Great numbers of people had collected in the churchyard and a few minutes before noon the corpse was brought out through the eastern gate of the garden leading into the churchyard...All the shops in Haworth were closed and the people filled every pew and the aisles in the church..."

The parson's body was lowered into the vault within the altar rails and placed beside the coffin of Charlotte. "Dr Burnet (Vicar of Bradford) signed the registers...Then he followed the last of the congregation out into the sunlight. Thus they left Patrick sleeping amidst the ashes of genius".

Patrick Bronte willed his estate to Mr Nicholls, "my beloved son-in-law", who now became aware of a special type of visitor, the souvenir-hunter, anxious to possess anything connected with the Brontes. The sorrowful Nicholls was so upset at the thought of strangers laying hands on family treasures that when a new tablet to the family was placed in Haworth Church, he had the two former tablets (Charlotte's name appeared on a separate tablet) taken to the Parsonage garden, where they were broken up and buried four feet deep.

Nicholls was keen to take over the incumbency, but the local people were "agin it". So he left, and with him all the objects specifically associated with Charlotte, Emily and Anne—manuscripts, drawings, even clothing.

Nicholls settled in Ireland, where the Bronte story had begun with the birth of Patrick, and he took up farming. He married his cousin but Charlotte was rarely far from his mind; they honeymooned in the same Irish haunts he had visited with his first wife!

He died, aged 89, in 1906. It is said that the last word he uttered was "Charlotte".

Back at Haworth, the name of Charlotte Bronte was on the lips of visitors thronging the Bronte haunts. The ever-obliging sexton continued to retail stories of the family. W H Cooke (1868) was shown the Bronte pew, "which is close before the altar". Charlotte was so small, said the saxton, that she had a footstool. "Yes, the pew was in exactly the same state as when they sat in it. Ah, sir, I once saw Thackeray and an American, who, they tell me, is a great man over there, called Emerson, and Miss Martineau, and Miss Bronte, all sitting in that pew, one Sunday".

Mr Cooke and his companion were showed the marriage register, with the signatures of Mr Nicholls and Charlotte, written in the presence of Ellen Nussey and Margaret Wooler. "Having duly inscribed our names in the visitors'-book, which, we noticed, contained the names of persons from all quarters of the globe, we were taken out of the church into the churchyard, and shown the grave of old Tabby, the faithful servant. . ."

For a time, in the fast-changing Haworth, the Brontes were not often mentioned. Jackdaw, writing in the *Mercury Supplement* in 1896 about a visit to Haworth that had occurred some 30 years before, was depressed to find how completely they [the Brontes] all seemed to have passed out of the lives of their neighbours.

"It was considered strange that one should take the trouble to visit Haworth in order to see their last resting-place and the house where they had dwelt and worked in by-gone years".

On that winter day, Haworth Parsonage looked melancholy and deserted. The snow lay on the moors "and the leaden skies of winter loomed above my head. I know that it was with a feeling of profound depression that I left the place. Little did I think that thirty years after, the people of the West Riding, who had shown part indifference to the family of Charlotte Bronte during her lifetime, would be turning to Haworth as to a shrine, and that the slender memorials of that pure and noble life would be gathered together and treated as sacred objects".

In 1914, the village had a Bronte cafe and one of the little streets was known as Bronte Street. A newspaper correspondent mention that the street name was "written without the dots, the name being pronounced in one syllable, as it was by the villagers years ago and is by the old inhabitants still".

Some Haworth shops exhibited pictures of Charlotte, her father and studies of the old church. The correspondent added: "It is quite impossible to be in Haworth many minutes without being conscious of the Bronte spirit which pervades everything".

Top Withens, said to be the inspiration for "Wuthering Heights", was just one of many small moorland farmsteads.

Ponden "Kirk", an outcrop of weather-seamed gritstone on the
Bronte Moors (a drawing by T Mackenzie from "Bronte Moors and
Villages", by Elizabeth Southwart (1923).

3. Creating a Legend
Mrs Gaskell's Biography

No quailing, Mrs Gaskell; no drawing back.
Patrick Bronte to Charlotte's biographer.

Mrs Gaskell was the first and greatest of the Bronte Legend-mongers.
Donald G Hopewell (1946).

ELIZABETH GASKELL, wife of a dissenting minister, mother and celebrated novelist, having been invited by Patrick Bronte to write a biography of his beloved Charlotte, took the old parson at his word when he urged her to be frank. She would not quail, neither would she draw back.

Mrs Gaskell had known Charlotte for some five years, since the day she received from her a copy of *Shirley,* written under the pseudonym of Currer Bell and had sent the shy young authoress an approving letter. They first met at the Lakeland home of the Kay-Shuttleworths.

Mrs Gaskell was invited to Haworth where, between six-inch shivers, for it was infinitely colder than Manchester, she became aware of the main aspects of an astonishing story of suffering, fortitude and courage.

Patrick Bronte, in asking Mrs Gaskell to write a biography of his beloved daughter, was putting her reputation in the hands of a writer with the ability to cause alarm among the reading public—she was outspoken and infused much of her work with social-realism—and who had no special love of him. She could not forgive him for neglecting to inform her of Charlotte's terrible last illness. Now she was to become Charlotte's "official" biographer.

Mr Bronte's concern was for Charlotte's image, which already— soon after her death—was becoming distorted by those who wrote about her after listening to village tittle-tattle. He wanted a biography that would be based on fact, as recalled by those who knew her and on written sources. The idea of a biography came from Charlotte's great friend, Ellen Nussey. Mr Nicholls's objections were over-ruled by Mr Bronte.

Mrs Gaskell, having been approached, joyfully obliged. Much moved by the tragic aspects of the life of this diminutive, shy and dowdy parson's daughter, she had already put the idea to her publisher (to "make the world...honour the woman as much as they have admired the writer") and was now having a chance to develop it with the co-operation of the father and Charlotte's closest friends.

The result was a biography with the strength and drama of a novel. Biographical material was there in abundance. For example, she was able to read at least 300 of about 500 letters which Charlotte had written to Ellen Nussey and which Ellen now made available for the biographer's scrutiny.

Mrs Gaskell appears to have made up her mind about Charlotte at an early stage. She would be projected in the best possible light, of course; nothing must besmirch her reputation. Reading the letters loaned by Ellen gave her "a very beautiful idea" of Charlotte's character.

The writer visited Haworth with Sir James Kay-Shuttleworth in whose august presence Mr Bronte and Mr Nicholls readily permitted items of interest to be collected for biographical reference. Sir James even arranged for Mrs Gaskell to send a photographer from Manchester to Haworth to copy a much-admired portrait of Charlotte which belonged to Mr Nicholls.

Elizabeth Gaskell chatted with Charlotte's friends, visited the Bronte haunts in Yorkshire and Lancashire and crossed the North Sea to visit the Pensionnat Heger in Belgium. In her eagerness to present an unsullied Charlotte, she committed sins of commission and omission, including unsubstantiated gossip and excluding such important topics as Charlotte's love for M Heger, a love to which he does not appear to have responded, for while his wife refused to see the English visitor he allowed Mrs Gaskell to see letters written to him by Charlotte.

The Life of Charlotte Bronte was published in March, 1857, two years after Charlotte's death. As though sensing the impact her book would have, the authoress contrived to be on holiday in Italy when *The Life* reached the shops.

Mrs Gaskell wrote to Ellen Nussey, who had known Charlotte better than most: "And I weighed every line with all my whole power & heart".

So did the Rev W Carus-Wilson, founder of the Clergy Daughter's School at Cowan Bridge, where Charlotte had been so unhappy, portraying the conditions with a grimness that had sent a shudder through readers of *Jane Eyre*. The clergyman now found the lightly-veiled and uncomplimentary impression of himself repeated in Mrs Gaskell's biography.

Every relevant line was also weighed by a certain Mrs Lydia Robinson, formerly of Thorpe Green Hall, near York, with whom Branwell Bronte had dallied. Their association was now mentioned in the enduring form of the printed page. Mrs Robinson, who had married for a second time and was now Lady Scott, threatened legal action. Mrs Gaskell's legal adviser and close friends framed the apology that appeared in *The Times,* the author being still abroad.

There was line-weighing at the humbler homes of the Haworthians and that of Nancy Malone (nee Garr), a former servant of the Brontes, now living in Bradford. (Her sister, Sarah, who also worked for the Brontes, had emigrated to America). Nancy told a writer in the *Leeds Mercury Supplement* of March 25, 1893, that nearly everything Mrs Gaskell had written about Mr Bronte was untrue or based on flimsy evidence.

Having read a few pages, she had gone over to Haworth to talk with Mr Bronte about the book. The old man, "though much perturbed, refused to trouble himself about the matter". Mrs Gaskell's assessment of him must have taken him by surprise. She had never taken to him, despite his courtesies towards her.

Mr Nicholls was displeased, having not favoured the proposal for a biography. To Mr Nicholls, the whole business was "a source of pain and annoyance".

Far from feeling that she owed a debt to Patrick Bronte for promoting the idea of a biography, Mrs Gaskell did not have much patience with him (he was that strange, half-mad husband whom Maria Bramwell had married) and her pen portrait was of a stern and eccentric man. He, with great generosity, did not speak an unkind word about her or the book. It was enough that someone of the literary standing of Mrs Gaskell had chronicled Charlotte's life.

Mrs Gaskell, returning from her holiday on May 28, was acquainted with the rumblings of discontent. Today, as we languidly read this fine book, we can imagine what a powerful impact it would have had on mid-Victorian society.

The Life was also a guide book. Novelists draw greatly on their imagination for people and places. Mrs Gaskell was the first major writer to fix the Brontes in specific, identifiable settings. Readers could not wait, having finished the book, to set off on a round of the Bronte haunts, both factural and fictional.

Mrs Gaskell's life in Manchester made her familiar with working class folk and their blunt speech. At Haworth, she found herself in an industrialised village where the people were inclined to be curt and their speech harsh.

Her prose had style, of course. Her first visit to Haworth had been on "a dull, drizzly Indian-inky day" in late September. She saw "poor, hungry-looking fields; stone fences everywhere, and trees nowhere".

Mrs Gaskell, unrepentant at the outcry caused by the publication of her major work, sardonically suggested that the third edition might hold an expression of regret "for having offered so expensive an article as truth to the public".

She visited Mr Bronte in November 1860; he received Mrs Gaskell and her daughter Meta in his bedroom. There was no softening of attitudes. Mrs Gaskell later wrote: "He is touchingly softened by illness; but still talks in his pompous way and mingles moral remarks and sometimes stale sentiments with his conversation on ordinary subjects".

As for Mr Nicholls, he was more unpopular in the village than ever, wrote Mrs Gaskell, "and seems to have even a greater aversion than formerly to any stranger visiting his wife's grave..."

4. The American Interest
Visits to Haworth

No other land furnished so many eager and enthusiastic visitors to the Bronte shrine as the United States, and the number of Americans who found their way to Haworth during the ten years immediately following the death of the author of *Jane Eyre* would, if properly recorded, astonish the world.
                    Sir Wemyss Reid, in a monograph on Charlotte.

THE AMERICAN element prevailed during the late summer and early autumn. William Sharp, writing in *The Pall Mall Magazine* of 1909, implied that the folk of Haworth had met so many Americans the local West Riding speech now had the twang of New England.

An American professor who was among the privileged folk permitted to enter the Parsonage—he called without having made an appointment—met Patrick Bronte, who displayed "real kindness of manner but with something of the stateliness of the old school. Short hair, white as the driven snow, ample cambric cravat completely covering his chin. Black dress of the most scrupulous neatness. Strong rugged features, high forehead and swarthy complexion. . . eyes partly closed but he is almost blind".

Patrick questioned his visitor on all aspects of American life, especially education, and then showed him round the parsonage, including the dining room, where a drawing of Charlotte by Richmond reposed in an oval frame; the image looked down on the table round which the sisters had walked and on the sofa where Emily had died. Martha took the American on a tour of the kitchen, with its open range and copper pans.

Charles Hale, from Boston, Massachusetts, visiting Haworth in November, 1861—the year of Patrick Bronte's death—left the village with souvenirs bought at the sale of Patrick's possessions, plus some actual fragments of the parsonage: Mr Bronte's bell-pull, "the whole lower sash of the window of Charlotte Bronte's bedroom", and a few panes of glass.

James M Hoppin, Professor at Yale, wrote about a meeting with Mr Bronte in *The Old Country: Its Scenery, Art and People* (1867). Hoppin attended Haworth Church, hearing sermons preached by Bronte and Mr Nicholls. The Church and its environs fascinated the professor. "All was hard, weather-worn stone, with nothing green or smiling; there was not a tuft of grass about the churchyard". He sat in the squire's pew near the pulpit, which was "hung with faded green baize".

At the parsonage, he chatted with Mr Bronte and was conducted to the "parlor" where Charlotte had done much of her writing. "Her books still lay on the table. There was a Bible of Emily's, and a much-worn copy of Mrs Gaskell's *Mary Barton,* presented by the authoress to Mrs Nicholls". This room's furnishings were "simple to severity", its only ornament being a bunch of broom-grass on the table.

"Martha [the family servant] then showed me into the kitchen for a moment. This had been Tabby's kingdom. Every thing was exquisitely neat, and the copper pans shone like gold. It was a snug, warm, crooning place; and it was not difficult to see the picture, on a dark winter eve, when the storms howled over the moor and rattled against the windows, of those bright-faced children crouching together around the fire, telling their strange stories, and living in a world created by themselves.

"Here Emily Bronte studied German, with her book propped up before her, while she kneaded dough. Now all are gone; and the old father, shutting up many things in his own impenetrable mind, was still living on alone, thinking more perhaps of meeting his children again in a sunless and sorrowless world, than of all their fame in this..."

Claude Meeker, United States Consul at Bradford, figured largely in the activities of early Brontephiles and took every opportunity of showing visitors round the Bronte haunts. In an article published in the *Cincinnati Times Star* of Ohio on February 14, 1895, Meeker observed "the fact that the Bronte Country is not on the route of the tourists, is off the main line of travel, and almost free from the hurrying men with the red guide books, may lend an additional interest to the statement that a large sprinkling of the pilgrims to the Bronte shrine are Americans.

"Many of these devotees are not highly cultured nor of fine literary tastes. Some of them pronounce the name as though it were spelt 'Bront', but neither of these facts detract from the tribute they pay to genius."

He then became guide-bookish: "There are many ways of reaching Haworth, from many points. You can start from Bradford or Leeds and reach it by rail in a short time but if the reader cares to see a picturesque and charming country and to enter into the romance and sentiment of the occasion, let him take an hour or two in mid-summer and drive the ten or twelve miles."

Mr Meeker's first visit by this route was as escort to a party of ladies, including the wife of a representative abroad of the United States government. "She has since declared, though she has visited historic places in Great Britain and on the Continent, though she has lingered at the tombs of great men—authors and statesmen, she has never been so impressed as with this drive through Yorkshire hills and dales and the sight of the barren and bleak old-world village".

Mr Meeker did not restrict himself to Haworth; he knew all about Thornton, where some of the Bronte children were born. He had discovered that many of the residents had little trinkets and mementoes from the birthplace. "A gentleman residing at Thornton offered us an extra inducement beyond the well understood age and quality of his wine, and fame of his Sunday roast of beef. It was a sight of the genuine stone font at which Charlotte Bronte was christened".

Tourism was incomplete without victuals. Mr Meeker recommented a visit to the old inn near the church at Haworth, where you might be served with a rare roast of beef cooked on a jack before the open fire. He recommended the "old port" and "in the season you would do wrong if you omitted to order one of the hostess' bilberry pies or tarts, rich in red juices beyond my power of language to describe".

The Bronte name was revered in Texas where, in 1873, the first women's club in the state was devoted to perpetuating their memory. It began as a literary society in Mrs Viola Case's Seminary for Young Ladies. Five years later its scope was broadened to include married women in its membership. Its purpose was now defined as "the study of literature, the arts and travel".

Haworth Church had acquired a stained glass window commemorating the Brontes; it was the gift of an anonymous American (revealed to be George W Childs). Mr Meeker moistened the eyes of his readers when he wrote: "I am not a hero nor heroine worshipper but there were traits of character in this remarkable family of wild moor flowers calculated to attract the attention of any investigator.

"They were themselves like their favourite plant. The moor flower is short-lived. It shows signs of life late in the spring and is one of the first, exposed on the hilltops as it is, to feel the effects of blighting frost.

"Born on the moors, the six Bronte children's lives were as comparatively short as that of their favourite heather. Death has its hand on them while yet at school—transplanted plants—and ere the autumn of life was reached, all were gone".

By 1914, when thousands of visitors a year trudged along the moorland paths, the Americans were reported to be great pluckers of heather, which they posted to relatives and friends across the Atlantic. One enterprising American became rich through selling "Bronte heather".

Though now outnumbered by the Japanese, the Americans still impress by their single-minded determination to make the most of a stay in Bronteland. In 1965, an American woman persuaded the curator, Joanna Hutton, to show her round the Parsonage at 7 a.m. on a Sunday morning.

It was her ambition to visit the building in the small hours. She arrived in Harrogate on tour and prevailed on a sleepy hire-car driver to take her to Haworth for £14. In Haworth, at dawn, she could not get a reply at the Parsonage, so she enlisted the help of the local policeman; they turned up just as Mrs Hutton had returned to bed with a cup of tea after seeing her husband and son off for a day's sailing at Scarborough.

The American had her tour of the Parsonage—seven hours before the official opening.

5. Call of the Moors
Quest for "Wuthering Heights"

From the very back of the church rise the wild moors—the clouds
and moors seeming in truth almost to merge themselves in one at
the back of the sacred edifice.

W H Cooke (1868).

The moors...sombre, sweeping slopes of black rock, rough pale
grass and tough heather...

Phyllis Bentley.

THE BRONTE MOORS have shrunk! To the Victorian readers of
Wuthering Heights, they were vast and wild. It was here that the
wuthering wind made the old thorns creak and put ice crystals in the
bloodstream of warm-blooded creatures.

Victorian visitors like the American James M Hoppin (1867) wrote
of "rolling, dismal moorlands, without the sign of human habitation"
adding that "a month later, and these moors would be gorgeous with
heather blossoms".

To Charlotte Bronte, mention of the North brought to mind "a lonely moor" which was silent, still and trackless. Modern visitors going
to the moors pass an ice cream van and use boot-flattened tracks to
the Bronte Waterfall (where water trickles rather than rushes down
a gritstone staircase) on their way to Top Withens, one of many little
farms which, in Bronte days, gave the moorland tract a lived-in appearance.

Emily Bronte needed the Moors. Her great work, *Wuthering
Heights,* was, through Heathcliff, a celebration of such elemental
forces as might be found in nature on a storm-rent tract of moorland.

Top Withens is generally considered to have been the inspiration for
the farmstead of the Earnshaws. The novel indicates their home was
on a much larger scale—something like Law Hill, Southowram, near
Halifax, where Emily taught during the 1836-7 winter.

39

The tattered ruins of Withens and its companion trees, leaning with the prevailing wind, are a powerful Bronte symbol. For many years, reaching Top Withens was the destination of dedicated Bronte fans, who set off from Haworth with something of the excitement now felt by those who go to the headwaters of the Amazon.

Today, the path is well-defined; the ruins were "consolidated" in 1980 and they no longer impress. A reader of the *Keighley News* thought they "resemble a giant sheep dip calculated to destroy any fictional association with the Brontes".

The Victorian world of letters was shaken by *Wuthering Heights,* which the 29-year-old Emily (under the pseudonym Ellis Bell) saw in its printed form in 1847, a few months before her death from tuberculosis.

Emily introduced a monster into English literature in the form of Earnshaw, whose brutish behaviour drew from Isabella Linton the question: "Is Mr Heathcliff a man?"

Top Withens, this solitary, wind-plucked farmhouse and adjacent barn standing at an elevation of rather more than 1,300 ft., was too small to contain Heathcliff, but does provide a satisfying skyline destination for Bronte pilgrims who do not mind walking a few miles by moor and gill.

In high summer, the ling is empurpled with bloom; the thorns at the moor edge, and the deciduous trees in the clough (pronounced cloo) bear foliage in 1,000 shades of green. Black flies torment people and animals. Black beetles lumber through the mini-jungle of heather and grasses.

Autumn sees the bracken fronds turn into a coppery hue which, with the wizened moor grasses, give the moors a russet hue. Winter streaks them with snow; and then it is spring, surely the Bronte girls' favourite season, when the sheep brighten their nose-ends while pulling at the moorcrop (the early stage of cotton-grass).

Cock grouse shout *kowa, kowa, kowa.* Larks sing as they ascend and pipits chitter as they descend, stiff-winged, stiff-tailed, in their territorial "shuttlecock" flight. A cock ring ouzel, the northern nightingale, gives its fluty song. The curlews glide and call. . .

The Haworth moors are small by Pennine standards or by those of North-East Yorkshire. In Bronte times, despite the presence of many

Continued on page 49.

The Parsonage, viewed from the churchyard and the stone setts.

Two drawings from "A Picture History of Yorkshire", by J S Fletcher (1899). Above—Keighley, the manufacturing town through which most visitors to Haworth passed. Below—Haworth Old Church and Parsonage.

Above—Rev Patrick Bronte and Dr William Cartman.
Below—Haworth Old Rectory.

HAWORTH OLD RECTORY.

Above—Haworth Main Street. Below—Kitchen at the Bronte Parsonage Museum.

Above, left—Sign outside the Black Horse, Haworth. Right—A walker beside the track from Haworth to Top Withens. Below—Japanese visitors come under the gaze of moorland sheep at Top Withens.

For the Big Screen

Bronte-ising a barn near Grassington for a Paramount production of "Wuthering Heights". A field barn becomes a church and wood and plaster tombstones appear in an adjacent croft.

CATHY AND HEATHCLIFF ON THE MOORS

In the autumn of 1991, the British Wool Marketing Board, based in Bradford, took Cathy and Heathcliffe to Tokyo, as part of a British fair held in the large Mitsukoshi store. The store had requested that a short presentation, based on Emily Bronte's "Wuthering Heights", which is a firm favourite with the Japanese, who are familiar with the romantic 1930's Hollywood version, should include drama, music and dance. Pictured here, in a Haworth setting, before their departure for Japan, are Paul Henry, as Heathcliff, and Mrs Ann Lloyd, a radiographer from Shipley, who played the part of Cathy.

EDGE OF THE MOOR

One of the signposts on Haworth Moors has a Japanese sub-title, which simply means "footpath". The discs relate to colour-coded routes in the Bronte Country. Haworth, which receives many thousands of Japanese visitors annually, has produced a guide book written in Japanese. There is no English edition of this work!

small moor-edge farms, they were wild, elemental, the playground of storms and the haunt of strange beings.

The report of a Parliamentary inspection of Haworth in 1850 mentioned "a very extensive tract of moorland . . . which extends far and wide to the south west, with nothing to relieve the unbroken surface of bog and peat, excepting at the end next to Haworth, where huge hollows and vast spoil heaps, mark the spots at which it has been very extensively worked for flagstones and ashlar blocks".

These were the Penistone Quarries, where now the summer sun brings a responsible sparkle from visitors' cars.

Early this century, the Haworth Moors were frequently referred to as the Bronte Moors, and the falls at Harbour Springs were being called the Bronte Falls. A nearby stone, fashioned in an L-shape, became known as the Bronte Chair.

They were but incidental features on the steady climb to Top Withens, the Brontean highspot. In 1964, a procession of members of the Bronte Society wended its way along that route and a plaque was placed on the remains of the old farmstead. The plaque has the following inscription:

Top Withens
This farmhouse has been associated with
Wuthering Heights
the Earnshaw Home in Emily Bronte's Novel.
The buildings, even when complete, bore
no resemblance to the house she described,
but the situation may have been in her
mind when she wrote of the moorland
setting of the Heights.

The *Keighley News* correspondent considered "it may be the means of attracting many more visitors during the coming months to this former lonely outpost, where men toiled long and earnestly to eke out a livelihood from the surly acreage".

He speculated that Emily may have had this "gaunt building" in mind when she wrote:

There is a spot mid barren hills
Where winter howls and driving rain;
But if the dreary tempest chills,
There is a light that warms again.
The house is old, the trees are bare.
Moonless above bends twilight's dome;
But what on earth is half so dear —
So longed for—as the hearth of home?

The setting is right for *Wuthering Heights*—wuthering being "a significant provincial adjective, descriptive of the atmospheric tumult to which its station is exposed in stormy weather"—but compare the modest farmstead of Top Withens with Lockwood's description in the novel and you will soon realise that Emma was thinking of a grander place.

The Haworth moors are a man-made feature of a landscape which previously was covered with scrubland. The open conditions and prevalence of heathers are maintained by systematic firing of the rank growth to encourage new shoots—fresh food for grouse and sheep.

Generations of small-time farmers "took in" the moor and created a web of drystone walls, made by breaking up the gritstone outcrops. Through hard physical toil they improved the "intakes" until oblongs of green stood out against the dun colours of the remaining moorland.

Top Withens (which some call High Withens and the signposts refer to as Withins) was simply one of the moorland farms of 17th and 18th century date where people had to "scrat for a living". The ruined Dean Side Farm, not far from the Bronte Falls, was once a prosperous place, nicknamed 'T'Jobbing Shop' because it was tenanted by men nicknamed Will o' Jobbings and Jim o' Jobbings who, in addition to farming, repaired farm and household inplements.

At a time when there were a few large families, nicknames proliferated and amused the visitors to "Bronteland". Sam o' Bills (a Greenwood from Stanbury) dug coal at South Dean. It was poorish stuff, hard and brittle, but a fire made from it was known to last a long time. Sam o' Bills, having broken the law, made up his fire before he set off for prison, a judge having insisted that he should spend 14 days there. On his return home, Bill is said to have found the fire was still burning.

Every self-respecting tourist found his or her way to Top Withens. (Lower and Middle Withens were also seen; these were demolished in the 1920s). Some visitors called to see Timmy Feather, "the last of the handloom weavers" at Stanbury.

Whiteley Turner, in his book entitled *A Spring-time Saunter round and about Bronteland* (1913), records meeting a solitary walker who directed him to "Higher Withens", commenting that "there's nubdy lives et ony o' th'buildin's naah". The farmhouse was said to stand "under th' 'ill edge . . . Ther'is a bit of a sign of a track forrard, but it's sooa faynt yo'll 'av ta booath put yo'r specs on an' strike matches ta find it".

Whiteley Turner quoted from Emily's novel: "One may guess the power of the north wind blowing over the edge by the excessive slant of a few firs at the end of the house, and by a range of gaunt thorns, all stretching their limbs one way, as if asking alms of the sun. Happily the architect had foresight to build it strong, the narrow windows are deeply set in the wall, and the corners defended with large jutting stones".

Turner saw that "the building before us comprises mistal, barn, house—which at one time had a thick coating of plaster—and peat-house, substantially and firmly planted end-on to the hill-side . . . The narrow windows are deeply set in the wall. The panes originally were evidently leaded and diamond-shaped, for a last remnant hangs partly torn from a mullion. We peer through this opening, knowing the place is unoccupied, and behold a weird hearth".

They also observed "a rudely-constructed table and seats, a dinted enamelled kettle, and heaped-up ashes in the rusty grate suggest occasional visits by shepherds. Crouching in the cramped house porch we try the door, but find it securely fastened as are also those of the barn and mistal. Access is only possible to the lofty peat-house, now serving as shelter for moorland sheep.

"There appears to be no date on the building. Across the yard, where grass springs up between the rough pavement, are two tiny fenced strips—probably sheep folds, but suggesting an old-time garden—at the top of which a group of young sycamores bend their

slender limbs northwards, as if imploring mercy from the elements. . .
We would fain linger, but time forbids, and the wind blows chill''.

Twenty minutes' walk from ''Wuthering Heights'' the hikers reached the summit of the moor at 1,457 feet. ''On our right is Withens
Height (1,500 feet). Not a habitation or soul within sight. On every
hand nothing but wild waste''. The sharp whistle they heard was not
the call of a moor bird but, almost certainly, the shriek of an engine
at the reservoir works in the valley.

In 1923, when ''Higher Withens'' was visited by Elizabeth
Southwart, the house was occupied by ''a solitary man, a discharged
soldier trying to regain his health.

''Every day he creeps down below to seek his fellows, and
sometimes stays there all day, for that solitude is too much for any
human being who has not sought it voluntarily''.

In a wilder part of the moor lies Ponden Kirk—the Penistone Crag
of *Wuthering Heights*—being part of the gritstone edge that has been
sculpted by wind and rain until, at one point, a hole remains through
which Victorian spinsters tried to squeeze. Those who succeeded
could look forward to a wedding.

Patrick Bronte found inspiration on the moors; he also wrote vividly
about a bog-burst, from a surfeit of rain, which he insisted in calling
an ''earthquake''. Startled observers at Ponden Kirk saw a waterfall
of mud descending into the valley. Normally, there is little water to
be seen here, but a lively waterfall forms after heavy rain.

This, rather than the so-called Bronte Falls, must have been the
waterfall visited by Charlotte and her husband shortly before her
death. It needed a special effort, which is more than can be said for
the Bronte Falls. Norman Raistrick, custodian of the Parsonage
Museum at the time, mentioned that a local photographer had temporarily improved these when he wanted to take photographs for
postcards; he built small dams to heighten the dramatic effect.

6. The Bronte Society
Order out of Chaos

The Society acts as guardian to letters, writings and personal
belongings of the Bronte family, and these treasures are housed in
the Parsonage Museum.

From the Museum brochure.

WHEN the Bronte Society was 50 years old, the president, Donald G
Hopewell, related how and why it was formed. He cited the legends
and the wild surmise and ill-based assumptions which cropped up as
soon as the Brontes became famous.

Such misleading impressions continued even after Mrs Gaskell
published *The Life of Charlotte Bronte*. Mrs. Gaskell perpetuated
stories which had no foundation in fact. The welter of apocryphal
family history and crude fairy tales became "so fantastic that the
least critical of Bronte worshippers became suspicious".

The Bronte Society, with its mission to give an authentic account of
Bronte life and literary activity, had a timely birth. Not only was it
to correct mistaken ideas about the Brontes, but through research and
scholarship it gave the Brontes their proper perspective in the literary
world.

W W Yates, a Dewsbury journalist who had long taken an interest
in the Brontes and their books, was the first to suggest in print that
a Bronte Society should be formed. His note was published in *The
Leeds Mercury* on November 25, 1893, and followed the recent
publication of Dr Wright's book *The Brontes in Ireland,* which had excited interest in the family. Had not the time arrived, wrote Mr Yates,
to make an effort to secure, and to preserve for the use of the public
for ever, the literary and other relics of Charlotte and her sisters?

A necessary preliminary to all this was the establishment of a
Bronte Society to collect information about the family and particularly the sisters. Such a Society would "arrange for the taking of

photographs of places on a scale to be selected by the committee, as, for instance, is being done just now for Warwickshire [Shakespeare Country]''.

The Bronte Society was formed at a meeting in the Council Chamber at Bradford Town Hall on December 16, 1893, when the Headmaster of Bradford Grammar School, the Rev W H Keeling, presiding in the absence of the Mayor, said that the Brontes, though not of Yorkshire parentage, represented the true Yorkshire spirit. They depicted the lovely Yorkshire scenery. They formed a strong link between Yorkshire and the world of literature.

Mr Yates returned to the theme of a museum to house drawings, manuscripts, paintings and personal relics, editions of the works of the Bronte sisters and books relating to them. These suggestions were adopted. In the first year, the number of members of The Bronte Society rose to 156.

Living links remained with the Brontes. Charlotte's husband, the Rev A B Nicholls, her great friend Ellen Nussey, the Rev J C Bradley, one of the curates referred to in *Shirley,* and old residents with sharp minds, were available for first-hand accounts of the Parsonage family.

A museum established in upper rooms at the Yorkshire Penny Bank, Haworth, was opened by Sir John Brigg on May 18, 1895, on which day special trains were laid on from surrounding towns. Haworth's principal buildings were bedecked with flags. After a grey morning, the sun appeared. Bandsmen played rousing music at the top of the main street, the flagstones of which had been cleaned for the occasion.

Smith, Elder and Company had loaned to the museum trustees the manuscripts of *Jane Eyre* and *Villette.* These and many other objects attracted almost 10,000 visitors in the first few months. Ellen Nussey, a personal friend of Charlotte, found but one flaw with the labelling of the exhibits. A portrait by Charlotte was not of Emily, as stated, but of Anne.

In 1905, a special service was held at Haworth to commemorate the 50th anniversary of the death of Charlotte Bronte. Hymns composed by Charlotte and Anne were sung and the Rev S Bickersteth, Vicar of Leeds, preached an unmemorable sermon, from the Epistle to the

Hebrews: "Let us therefore labour to enter into that rest".

A letter from the wife of the Rev Nicholls gave an update on his health. He was in his 89th year and though infirm and weakly suffered little pain and went out every day. "We read for him but only things of common interest. We never give him letters or anything likely to excite him or set him thinking".

In Guiseley on December 29, 1912, there was a service to commemorate the centenary of the marriage of Rev Patrick Bronte and Maria Branwell.

For its 21st annual meeting, the Society returned to Dewsbury, where the Vicar was quick to point out that Patrick Bronte's connection with the West Riding began here with his appointment as curate.

The Vicar had been "away at school" when Patrick Bronte died in 1861, but he remembered what excitement was caused by the news, and what a rush there was to the libraries for the works of the Bronte sisters. He caught the infection and read *Shirley* for the first time; it had been a favourite ever since.

Five hundred people attended the meeting. A C Benson, speaking on the Message of Charlotte Bronte to the 19th century, was—as he termed it—"critically sympathetic".

W W Yates challenged the Mrs Gaskell image of Patrick Bronte as "rather a hard" man. From what Yates had heard from the old people who remembered him, he was indeed "a very kind man and beloved by the people amongst whom he lived".

It was reported that during the 20 years of its existence, the museum collection had been richly augmented and, despite the fact that members of the Society were admitted free of charge, over £670 had been taken in admission fees. "A charge of threepence is made for admission, which represents an aggregate attendance of 54,000".

The Society continues to nourish scholarship and uses the Transactions and its extensive library as a repository of related material. The social aspect continues to be fostered through an annual literary luncheon, coach excursion, walk and by inviting eminent speakers to talk about the Brontes.

7. The Bronte Relics
And Mr Wise the Forger

Any relic or manuscript connected with the wonderful sisters and
their wayward brother...is at once seized upon by an adoring sect.
The Daily Telegraph, May 30, 1914.

THE death of Charlotte, after her short-lived celebrity as an author,
stimulated interest in relics of the family. Those who had lived or
worked at the Parsonage were in the best position to acquire mementoes of the Brontes.

The first sale of Bronte relics took place at Saltaire in 1886 and consisted of items which had belonged to Martha Brown, servant at the
Parsonage. Here were letters from Charlotte to Martha and from
Thackeray to Patrick Bronte. Martha had also preserved pencil and
water-colours by members of the Bronte family.

Harwood Brierley, writing in 1893 about Mr Feather, a Haworth
watchmaker, related how just after Charlotte's death he was visited
by Mr Nicholls, the widower, who handed over a clipping of her hair
which he wished to have put into a ring. A few hours later, Mr
Nicholls returned, asking for the hair, anxious that Mr Feather should
not lose it—or substitute one lock of hair for another!

Nancy Malone (nee Garrs), a former servant living in Bradford,
showed her Bronte relics to two visitors in 1893. They subsequently
wrote a newspaper article in which was mentioned a framed letter
from Patrick, testifying to the sisters' [Nancy and Sarah's] kind and
honest nature. In view of Mrs Gaskell's assertion in *The Life* that the
servants had been "wasteful", Mr Bronte had included a note that
this was not the case!

Nancy "drew forth [from a drawer] a little roll, which she handled
so tenderly and reverently that we almost guessed what it contained.
It was a letter from Charlotte Bronte". Nancy had been offered £5 for

it, but—though not well off—had refused. The letter, dated July, 1845, had not been considered of great importance to anyone but Nancy, Charlotte having mentioned the "kindly sentiments" which the Brontes cherished "towards the humbler members of their household".

The death of Ellen Nussey in 1897 released many Bronte relics. At the sale of Ellen's household effects, one man bought an old leather case, the type intended to hold a watch and trinkets. On a piece of cardboard within the case was found a water-colour painting of young Emma, the artist being almost certainly Charlotte Bronte. Such was the opinion of experts at the National Portrait Gallery.

In 1905, Whiteley Turner, on his *Springtime Saunter,* met a Mrs Radcliffe whose maiden name was Tabitha Brown. She was the daughter of John Brown, sexton at Haworth Church for two decades. Tabitha's sister, Martha, who assisted the more famous Tabitha, servant of the Brontes, was only 10 years old when she began work at the Parsonage.

Martha had acquired the Bronte mementoes when the contents of the Parsonage were dispersed following the death of Patrick Bronte. Martha had in turn passed them down to Mrs Radcliffe and Turner was astonished to discover that some of them might be purchased, if the offer was satifactory.

Turner saw "a row of brass candlesticks there on the mantelpiece"; they once adorned that of the kitchen at Haworth Parsonage. Turner and his companion were shown Anne's work box, containing "a faded and mother-eaten needle-case containing an assortment of needles, etc., all rusty and useless". Also belonging to Anne was a "delicate and oval-shaped brooch" and they were permitted to hold the "plaited hair of Charlotte..."

Most of the relics owned by Mrs Ratcliffe had been loaned to the Bronte Society to be exhibited in the museum. A niece of Mrs Ratcliffe, known as Miss Binns, had loaned the dress which Charlotte wore on her honeymoon.

Messrs R and F Brown, booksellers at Haworth and Keighley, saw commercial possibilities in exhibiting Bronte relics and consequently they augmented their own modest collection with a much larger one purchased from Alfred Gledhill, of Keighley, in 1889. The Browns opened a Museum of Bronte Relics as an adjunct to their *Temperance Hotel* in Haworth Main Street. (It was not so much a hotel as refreshment rooms; the museum occupied an upper room).

The collection included paintings, drawings and specimens of needlework (the working of silk) by Charlotte. Among the paintings was the now familiar one of Floss, the Bronte dog, in pursuit of a grouse on the moors.

A letter from Charlotte to "Dear Susey", a family friend, was dated June 13, 1848, and included these words: "If ever you feel troubled about anything you will not forget who is your best help and guide in every difficulty, and, separated as you are for a little while from your earthly friends, you will humbly and faithfully entreat the protection of your Friend and Father who is in heaven".

A copy of the *Quarterly Review* of December, 1848, contained an article on *Vanity Fair* and *Jane Eyre* in which the writer referred to Charlotte as having "horrid taste". It is said that when she had read this note, Charlotte wept bitterly and took to her bed.

The brothers Brown added to their collection some relics belonging to William Scruton, a Bradford antiquary. The Browns made an offer of £8, considering this was "ample value for them and as much as we can really afford to give, as we do not intend to make merchandise of them..." Scruton held out for £10 and received this sum.

Choice items from the Browns' museum and other relics were exhibited at Thornton in the autumn of 1890. The list included Branwell's oil painting of William Brown, "late sexton for 20 years of Haworth Church during the ministry of the Rev P Bronte".

Visitors saw Branwell's chair which had stood in the *Black Bull* at Haworth. On view were Charlotte's portfolio containing drawings given to Martha Brown, also her drawing-books and an autograph copy of *Jane Eyre* presented to Martha Brown. The Browns' advertisement for the exhibition mentioned Charlotte's "shawl, shoes, &c".

The Browns' enterprise at Haworth failed mainly because when their museum was opened, the Old Church was being demolished and the number of visitors to Haworth had declined. The effect of the reconstruction work at the church and Parsonage was mentioned by Harwood Brierley in the *Yorkshire Weekly Post* of January 8, 1887.

Brown's Refreshment Rooms

AND

MUSEUM OF BRONTË RELICS,

123, MAIN STREET, HAWORTH.

Large Refreshment Rooms for Clubs, Schools and Picnic Parties.

The following is a list of Views and Photographs of Haworth and the Brontë family, Cabinets, 1/1 ; Cartes-de-visites, 7d., post free

Rev. P. Brontë.
Rev. W. Grimshaw.
Mr. Nichols.
The Interior of the Old Church.

General View of Haworth.
Charlotte Brontë.
The Old Church.
The New Church.

[P. BRONTË].

The Brontë Group.
The Old Pew.
The Old Pulpit.
The Tablet.
Old Parsonage.

The Brontë Waterfalls.
The faithful servant, Martha Brown.
Charlotte's favourite dog, Floss.

Visitors to Haworth should not fail to see the Collection of BRONTË RELICS, which is the largest that has ever been got together.

Also a Pamphlet, by the Rev. P. Brontë, entitled : **Two Sermons and a Phenomenon,** or an account in verse of the Extraordinary Disruption of a Bog (better known as the Crow-hill Flood), which took place on the moors of Haworth on the 2nd day of September, 1824.—*Price 6d., post free 7 stamps.*

X

At the *Black Bull,* where formerly two hundred visitors had sat down to a Sunday dinner, "we were struck by the fact that no strangers seemed to be about".

In March, 1893, one of the brothers took the relics with him to the Chicago Exhibition, intending to exhibit them and then to sell them. This venture, like the earlier ideas, was not successful.

As interest in Bronte relics grew, on each side of the Atlantic, faking became commonplace. Donald Hopewell, in his presidential talk to the Bronte Society in 1946, observed: "At one time, Bronte cradles were so plentiful that Mrs Bronte must have had a new one for each of her babies; while Bronte pianos came so often on the market there must have been at least one such instrument in every room in the Parsonage...".

The formation of the Bronte Society and the opening of its first museum, in 1897, provided a repository for Bronteana which would be preserved for its own sake.

The effects of the late Ellen Nussey were featured in a sale at Birstall in May, 1898. These were mainly books. In some of the works written about the Brontes, Miss Nussey had made marginal notes. Sarcastic comments were added to a copy of Dr Wright's *Brontes in Ireland* and Bayne's *Two Great Englishwomen.*

A gold brooch which had belonged to Charlotte and held locks of hair from Emily and Anne had come into Ellen Nussey's collection as a gift from Patrick. At the sale, it was bought by James Miles, the Leeds bookseller.

In July, 1898, the Robinson Brown collection of Bronteana was sold at Sothebys. This consisted of objects which had been exhibited in past times by the Brown brothers. Most of the items had been Bronte gifts to Mr Brown's father, William, sexton at Haworth Church during 20 years of Patrick's incumbency and to his niece, Martha.

Gifts were received from Bronte collectors, especially from Thomas James Wise (1859-1937), who blemished an otherwise outstanding reputation as a Bronte scholar by allowing his enthusiasm to become a mania, adding to his passions as collector, bibliographer and editor those of forger and thief.

Wise, a South Country businessman who took up book-collecting as a hobby, was soon providing libraries and collectors with material connected with Victorian authors, including the Brontes. Wise was at his peak of activity around the turn of the century, collaborating with Clement King Shorter (who, with C W Hatfield, was also much respected for his scholarship).

When Bronte manuscripts came into the hands of "Tommy" Wise, he made up neat little packets of assorted items which had a ready sale. He did the Bronte cause a disservice by destroying the chronology and inter-relationships of important papers.

The man who published over 50 bogus pamphlets of eminent Victorian authors, each edition pre-dating the earliest known, was also implicated in the theft of the manuscripts of 17th century plays from the British Museum. His mis-deeds were systematically exposed through inquiries extending from 1934 until 1957.

Clement Shorter, having "become possessed" of a batch of letters penned by Charlotte Bronte, and anxious to secure the copyright, sailed to Ireland with his friend Robertson Nicholl, intent on meeting the Rev Arthur Bell Nicholls, the possessor of much Bronte material.

Shorter made a timely visit, for Nicholls, who had taken up farming and was married again, had come upon straitened times. Among the bargains was a brown-paper parcel containing letters written by the young Brontes and those strange little manuscript books in which Charlotte and Branwell had recorded the affairs of imaginery worlds. It seems that Nicholls, counting them of little value, had even considered burning them.

Shorter paid £400 for this parcel of material and by the time it came into the hands of Wise, the price had risen to well over £1,000. Shorter insisted on retaining the copyright. Wise promptly vandalised the material, putting some of it in expensive binders for sale to wealthy collectors in Britain and America. Other items were retained and the rest of the collection was sold off in the London second-hand book trade.

By printing material in small editions and giving it an early date, Wise exploited a form of literary forgery that was far simpler than trying to pass off hand-written material. For many years collectors did not associate the respectable and quiet-mannered Wise with such roguery.

In 1907 and 1914, Nicholls's second wife sent batches of Bronte documents to Sotheby's for sale. The first batch, which came on the market only a year after the clergyman's death, consisted mainly of books—some autographed by members of the family—from the Parsonage library. Also on sale were work-boxes belonging to the Bronte children and juvenile manuscripts. The sale realised £718.

Mrs Nicholls's second batch, offered in 1914, included some Brussels exercise books in German, French, and arithmetic, with corrections, believed to be in Professor Heger's handwriting. Now that a romantic attachment between Charlotte and Heger was being discussed in Bronte circles, any relevant scrap of paper was being "worshipped by a numerous cult" [*Daily Telegraph*].

In 1907, Sotheby's had on offer Charlotte's writing desk, paint box and samplers, along with a fragment of Napoleon's coffin given to her by M Heger. Three years later, a letter written by Charlotte in which she described her first meeting with Thackeray was sold. Charlotte, brave but naive, had written:

"The giant sat before me. I was moved to speak to him of some of his shortcomings—literary, of course. One by one his faults came into my mind, and one by one I brought them out and sought some explanation or defence. He did defend himself like a great Turk and heathen. That is to say, the excuses were often worse than the crime itself. The matter ended in decent amity. If all be well I am due at his house this evening".

Wise and Shorter were electrified in 1913 when letters written by Charlotte to Prof Heger of Brussels were handed over to the British Museum by Heger's son. The letters, written in French, were now translated into English and published in *The Times* of July 29.

The story of the intervention of Wise and Shorter is related by Wilfred Partington in *Thomas J Wise in the Original Cloth* (1946). *The Times* had asked M H S Spielman to translate the letters and he provided notes about them. On publication, Shorter had the temerity to protest to *The Times* about a breach of his copyright.

Wise said nothing but cashed in on the letters by surreptitiously publishing a "first edition" under the title *The Love Letters of Charlotte Bronte to Constantin Heger* (1914). No one concerned with the original publication in the newspaper seems to have been aware at the time of what he had done; and he had an explanation of sorts ready—that copyright in the letters was owned by his good friend Mr Shorter.

It appears to have been the last audacious act in the realm of Bronte relics. The 1914 sale of mementoes that had belonged to Mrs Nicholls consisted of 44 items, 41 being manuscripts and three articles of furniture. The whole realised £613 4s. The highest price, £105, was paid for Charlotte Bronte's draft manuscript of her fragment called *Emma*, which was bought by Bertram Dobell, bookseller.

As late as the 1930s, stories were circulating about American collectors paying fabulous prices but such stories were untrue and, by 1937, Bronte prices were dropping in New York, where any transactions in manuscripts were a useful barometer of interest to collectors everywhere.

Happily, Henry Houston Bonnell of Philadelphia owned the finest collection of Bronteana in private hands, for he gave it to the Bronte Society. It had been expected that this would be lodged in an American archive but Bonnell's widow interpreted her husband's desire as being the return of the material to Haworth and this was done in 1928-9.

The Bonnell Collection, which was catalogued meticulously by C W Hatfield, has a room at the Parsonage named after it and, as the catalogue proclaims, "it laid the foundation of what is now the largest Bronte archive in the world".

8. According to Virginia Woolf
Her first Published Piece

Haworth expresses the Brontes; the Brontes express Haworth; they fit like a snail to its shell.

Virginia Woolf

IN 1904, Virginia Stephens (later to be widely known by her married name Virginia Woolf) visited her cousin, Will Vaughan, his wife Madge and three children—Janet, Halford and Barbara—at Giggleswick School, in North Ribblesdale. He had been appointed headmaster.

Apart from the family re-union, she had at the back of her mind a visit to Haworth, stimulated by reading Mrs Gaskill's biography of Charlotte—though it was November, and the snow-dogs were howling around the Bronte moors.

The visit was made and the article appeared before the year's end in *The Guardian,* a London weekly newspaper appealing mainly to clerics.

Pale and drawn from her second nervous breakdown, Virginia won her doctor's approval for a visit to Giggleswick. Her sister Vanessa wrote to Will and Madge: "She is really quite well now—except that she does not sleep very well—and inclined to do too much in some ways. . .She ought not to walk very far or for a very long time alone. . .She goes to bed very early as I think you do and she is in all other ways absolutely normal in her doings".

With her unorthodox family background and strong feminist ideas, Virginia saw Madge as "like a starved bird up here". It was "quite pathetic" how eager she was to talk and "how full of ideas and theories—which have to be silenced the moment Will comes into the room, or he would call them morbid".

Virginia, travelling to Giggleswick by train, arrived in a cold snap of the type that characterises mid-November in the Dales. Writing to a friend on November 21, she related that she was "sitting at my window under the moors, which are all white with snow and frost, and the temperature is below freezing. I keep warm with a fire, and a fur rug, and I might be in the heart of the Alps. . ."

Virginia's reference to "we" suggests that she had the company of Madge, her cousin's wife, for the journey to Haworth. Virginia did not record the method of transport used and they presumably entrained at Giggleswick for Keighley, where she transferred to the Worth Valley line.

The blizzard had abated; she passed through "a very cheerful land, which might be likened to a vast wedding cake, of which the icing was slightly undulating; the earth was bridal in its virgin snow, which helped to suggest the comparison".

Keighley was assessed as being "hard and stony, and clattering with business, in the way of these Northern towns. They make small provision for the sentimental traveller, and our only occupation was to picture the slight figure of Charlotte trotting along the streets in her thin mantle, hustled into the gutter by more burly passers-by. It was the Keighley of her day and that was some comfort. . ."

So Virginia reached Haworth, "the shrine at which we were to do homage". She had the tourist's wonderment at the way Haworth straddles. "The houses, built of yellow-brown stone, date from the early nineteeth century. They climb the moor step by step in little detached strips, some distance apart, so that the town instead of making one compact blot on the landscape has contrived to get a whole stretch into its clutches".

Reaching the head of the street, she found the main objects of Bronte interest—church, parsonage, museum and school—within the proverbial stone-throwing distance. "The museum is certainly rather a pallid and inanimate collection of objects. An effort ought to be made to keep things out of these mausoleums, but the choice often lies between them and destruction, so that we must be grateful for the care which has preserved much that is, under any circumstances of deep interest".

Virginia lingered before a case containing "the little personal relics", Charlotte's dresses and shoes. "The natural fate of such things is to die before the body that wore them, and because these, trifling and transient though they are, have survived, Charlotte Bronte the woman comes to life, and one forgets the chiefly memorable fact that she was a great writer. Her shoes and her thin muslin dress have outlived her".

Virginia recalled that the old edition of Mrs Gaskell's Life had on its title-page a small sketch "which struck the keynote of the book; it seemed to be all graves—gravestones stood ranked all round; you walked on a pavement lettered with dead names; the graves had solemnly invaded the garden of the parsonage itself, which was as a little oasis of life in the midst of the dead.

"This is no exaggeration of the artist's, as we found: the stones seem to stare out of the ground at you in tall, upright lines, like an army of silent soldiers. There is no hand's breadth untenanted; indeed, the economy of space is somewhat irreverent. . . ."

Virginia noted that since the Brontes lived at the Parsonage, a new wing had been added. "It is easy to shut the eye to this, and then you have the square, boxlike parsonage, built of the ugly, yellow-brown stone which they quarry from the moors behind, precisely as it was when Charlotte lived and died there".

She saw nothing remarkable in a mid-Victorian parsonage, "though tenanted by genius". The only room which awakened her curiosity was the kitchen, now used as an ante-room, "in which the girls tramped as they conceived their work. One other spot has a certain grim interest—the oblong recess beside the staircase into which Emily drove her bulldog during the famous fight, and pinned him while she pommelled him. It is otherwise a little sparse parsonage, much like others of its kind".

The incumbent of 1904 allowed Virginia and her companion to look inside the Parsonage. "In his place," wrote Virginia, "I should often feel inclined to exorcise the three famous ghosts". Patrick Bronte's successor as parson at Haworth had swept away the body of the old church and replaced it with something more elaborate, in the manner of the later Victorians.

Virginia paid homage at the Bronte's last resting place and noted that the inscription placed beneath their names was "The sting of death is sin, and the strength of sin is the law, but thanks be to God which giveth us the victory through our Lord Jesus Christ". She referred to the aptness of the inscription and added that "however harsh the struggle, Emily, and Charlotte above all, fought to victory".

Back at Giggleswick, Virginia found life was rather "stuffy", adding: "Here we go on in the same way—endless tea parties of boys and masters, and now the old ladies of Giggleswick have taken to asking us out—so we are rather sociable".

Virginia married Leonard Woolf, himself no mean writer, who in *The Nation & Athenaeum* of May 12, 1928, reviewed with great perception the latest clutch of books, with special reference to Emily Bronte.

The Bronte Sisters, by Ernest Dimnet, a French critic, had first been published in French about 17 years earlier. This work "has the graceful sobriety characteristic of the French tradition in letters. Emily is one of those disorderly English geniuses for whom the French have naturally little understanding or appreciation, and it is, therefore, remarkable to find what a high place M Dinnet gives to her work".

Isabel C Clarke, author of *Haworth Parsonage, a Picture of the Bronte Family,* had produced what was in many ways "quite a good account of the lives and characters of the family", giving Emily her due, but was taken to task for treating hypotheses as facts.

Valentine Dobree, who wrote an introduction to a new edition of *Wuthering Heights,* was commended for showing "an admirable sympathy and subtlety in her criticism which will help those who want a guide to Emily Bronte's soul far better than all the hypothetical romances about the curate . . . or the most elaborate psychological reconstruction of the unfortunate Emily".

Leonard Woolf next considered *All Alone, the Life and Private History of Emily Jane Bronte,* by Romer Wilson, a book which "is almost as much about Miss Romer Wilson as it is about Emily Bronte, and the two seem to be not always completely distinguished in the author's mind".

So did the Brontes infiltrate Bloomsbury.

9. For Sale: One Parsonage
Sir James Foots the Bill

The field had evidently been set apart, and the founders of the church had said "in three-quarters of it we will inter the dead and in that other fourth we will bury the living."

Frank Peel (1855).

"I am one of the fast-narrowing circle of Haworth veterans who remember the Parsonage family."

Sir James Roberts, handing over the Parsonage
to the Bronte Society, 1928.

A FORMER custodian, Juliet Barker, described Haworth Parsonage to me as "a very simple house—austere on the outside, homely and comfortable within. The furnishings were inexpensive but always kept sparklingly clean. We take a great pride in keeping it in a pristine condition. We feel that is what the Brontes would have liked..."

The house was relatively new when the Brontes took up residence in 1820. When, 41 years later, the body of Patrick Bronte was borne to his place of burial, and the Bronte link with the Parsonage was snapped, it had become a "rotten old house", despite alterations and improvements made by Charlotte in mid-century. The Rev Wade, Bronte's successor re-styled the place and added a new wing.

As another long Pennine winter came grudgingly to a close, and the old building was silvered with frost, I stood in the churchyard and listened to the cawing of rooks—that most English of sounds—from the lofty trees. Every modern view of the parsonage includes trees. It is tempting to think of the Bronte girls being lulled to sleep by the soughing of the wind between the branches. Yet the trees are post-Bronte, being planted to help disperse the bodies in the graveyard, which was closed in Mr Bronte's time.

May Sinclair wrote that it is impossible to write of the three Bronte sisters, and forget the place in which they lived—"the black grey naked village, bristling like a rampart on the clear edge of the moor; the street, dark and steep as a gully, climbing the hill to the parsonage at the top; the small oblong house, naked and grey, hemmed in on two sides by a graveyard, its five windows, flush with the wall. . . ''

When built, the house was made to occupy a position well back on the site, so that a garden could be made. Emily, it seems, was ''head gardener''. The Bronte girls received flower seeds from their friend Ellen Nussey, including Sicilian peas and some crimson cornflowers.

The indispensable Mrs Gaskell noted that when Charlotte had her literary success, and more money to spend, she evidently refurnished the parlour. ''Everything fits into, and is in harmony with, the idea of a country parsonage, possessed by people of very moderate means. The prevailing colour of the room is crimson, to make a warm setting for the cold grey landscape outside''.

Frank Peel, visiting Haworth in the mid-19th century, recalled the Parsonage garden, which was small. You stepped straight off the graveyard into it. ''You also went down one step, as towards a larger grave. A flagged walk led up to the front door, and it was covered over with a damp green film, and in the interstices grew an almost black moss''.

Peel noted that ''the stone of the house was of the same melancholy tint as the flags of the walk: of all the sad, heart-broken dwellings I have passed this was the saddest''.

Mrs Gaskell's more cheerful note mentions not only the graveyard (''terribly full of upright tombstones'') but also a flower-border. In her time, servants did the work and ''everything about the house tells of the most dainty order, the most exquisite cleanliness. The doorsteps are spotless; the small old-fashioned window-panes glitter like looking-glass. Inside and outside of that house cleanliness goes up into its essence, purity''.

Standing at an elevation of some 1,000 ft above sea level, Haworth Parsonage catches every wind that blows. The Bronte Wind comes from the east. The family shuddered when they heard it blowing, for it usually heralded attacks of toothache and asthma.

The Parsonage must have been a cold house. The occupants suffered from the effects of the cold, which set off a facial twitching. It was assuredly a damp house and Aunt Branwell, who grew up in the temperate and sunny climate of Cornwall, kept pattens [clogs] on her feet, which were thus kept an inch or so above a damp, cold floor of Elland flags.

No direct reference has been found to what was burnt in the fireplaces. Presumably there was coal and also peat. Mr Bronte continually complained about the state of the chimneys. The room which became known as Mr Nicholl's Study was previously a peat-store, the main change being that an outside door was blocked and a door opened out from the body of the house.

In the 1850s, when fans came wonderingly to Haworth, Charlotte's alterations had been completed and she was married to Mr Nicholls. Charlotte's influence is strong. She stamped her personality on the Parsonage. Having been a governess, living in fine houses, she had developed ideas about what constituted good taste.

A detailed account of some principal rooms was written down by John Elliot Cairnes, of Trinity College, Dublin, who visited Haworth in September, 1858. He had hoped to meet Patrick Bronte, but the old parson was ill and had taken to his bed. He none the less hoped that Cairnes would "walk in & see the house".

Martha the maid showed him first the parlour. Charlotte's portrait was "on the dark side of the room", fronting a medallion cast of Branwell on the other, "while on either side of the door, there was the Duke of Wellington and Thackeray. There also was her little library, not above sixty or seventy vols in all but, with the exception of *Alison's Europe* (which I was sorry to see there) a most choice collection. . . ."

On the walls of "the old gentleman's study" were drawings of Charlotte and a watercolour by Emily of the dog Keeper, "with a cat and small dog". Martha mentioned Emily's courage in separating Keeper from other dogs when they were fighting. Mrs Gaskell had mentioned that she had pounded Keeper with her fists, but Martha could remember nothing about it. Cairnes suspected that Mrs Gaskell did not "scrutinize over carefully the authority of her stories, if they be only picturesque".

Cairnes was allowed to see some of "Charlotte B's" letters, "a small bundle of which, on my asking Martha if she had any, was produced. . . They were all addressed to Martha; generally commencing with some directions concerning household matters, and concluding with a brief description of where she was, what she was doing, & so forth.

They were in the gentlest and kindest vein, with an occasional dash of humour, but never passing beyond that which was perfectly natural in a Mistress, addressing her favourite maid''.

Mr Wade who succeeded Mr Bronte as incumbent of Haworth, incurred the wrath of the early pilgrims for carrying out alterations at the Parsonage. W H Cook (1868) referred to his ''execrably bad taste'' in removing the old-fashioned house windows and substituting brand-new plate glass ones ''of the most approved Regent-street construction''.

Cook thought that ''anything more utterly out of keeping with the rest of the surroundings than are these plate-glass windows it is impossible to conceive. Everything else about the house—always excepting those unfortunate plate-glass windows—is in unison with the weird, desolate scene which surrounds the parsonage''.

With the irascible Patrick Bronte dead and with Mr Nicholls farming in his native Ireland, visitors to the Parsonage were not as welcome as they had been. Cooke, after observing that the Parsonage seemed to consist of two rooms, one on each side of the house, spread himself in one majestic sentence:

''We say 'apparently consists', for we were not allowed to enter it— the present incumbent sternly refusing to admit a single visitor, or to permit one, even for an instant, to peer into that family sitting-room of the Brontes, wherein were written works which have conferred immortal lustre upon this incumbent's present residence, and which will live long after he himself has mouldered down to dust, and his bran-new [sic] window-frames have rotted to decay''.

Scant and bare was an impression conveyed by reminiscences of Charlotte published in *Scribner's Magazine* in 1871. ''There was not much carpet anywhere except in the sitting-room and on the study floor. The hall floor and stairs were done with sand-stone, always beautifully clean, as everything was about the house; the walls were not papered, but stained in a pretty dove-coloured tint; hair-seated chairs and mahogany tables, bookshelves in the study, but not many of these elsewhere . . .''

In 1897, Wade cordially received a party of members of the Bronte Society. Contrary to a popular view, which accounts that his restoration of the church and extension to the parsonage were designed to blur the Bronte image, "Mr Wade fully shares in the general admiration for the genius and character of the Brontes, and I am sorry to think it is not likely he will now put in print the stores of information he has accumulated during his long residence in the parish".

Except for an enlargement, the Parsonage in its main features was still as it had been in the time of the Brontes. "The old staircase has been retained, and I hope will always be retained. We stood once again in the room where Charlotte died. We heard how Patrick Bronte at that supreme hour appeared strong and stern, able to comfort and uphold the stricken husband, and how a little later he was found by a friend in his own room, kneeling in prayer, and shedding the tears of a great agony".

The Bronte Museum, in rooms above the Yorkshire Penny Bank, had been opened in 1897 and Hall's guidebook, published locally, mentions the Bronte Cafe in the main street as being "opposite the church and close to the Bronte Museum". Burra's luncheon and tea rooms were to be found in the main street "close to the Bronte museum and church".

Mr Hall informed readers that the ordinary way of getting to Haworth was by the Worth Valley branch—a single line, about five miles in length—and that cheap fares might be had from Bradford on Tuesdays and Saturdays and from Leeds on Wednesdays and Saturdays during the summer months. For the pedestrian, there were several more interesting routes...

Three old pennies secured admission to the Bronte Museum, where visitors gathered round the dress which Charlotte had worn on her honeymoon, or peered at Mr Bronte's spectacles and walking stick and the collar of Emily's dog Keeper.

At the annual meeting of the Bronte Society in 1927, when the entire cash assets of the society were just under 50, the exciting possibility of moving the Museum to the old Parsonage was the main talking point. Haworth Church Lands Trustees were prepared to sell the former home of the Brontes and, estimating that it would cost 3,000 to erect a suitable home for the Rector, gave a hint of the asking price.

It was suggested that a Carnegie Trust committee concerned with museums should be invited to visit Haworth, while others felt that funds should be raised locally. A newspaper report of this meeting was sent to Sir James Roberts who, with his wife, was abroad at that time. Lady Roberts, on being shown the cutting, saw this as a chance for her husband to do something for his native Haworth.

The career of James Roberts was the classic rise from rags to riches. The son of a Haworth farmer, he went to work in a mill at the age of 14. Six years later, his enterprise and hard work led him to be appointed manager. He started on his own account as a wool topmaker in 1873, and by 1882 he was able—with three associates—to buy the firm of Sir Titus Salt at Saltaire, the world's largest textile manufacturing business, which had just gone into voluntary liquidation.

By 1900, Roberts had become the sole owner; he became a baronet in 1909 and in the following year he demonstrated his status and considerable wealth by purchasing Strathallan Castle, in Perthshire. Ten years before he was invited to contribute to the purchase of Haworth Parsonage for the Bronte Society, he had sold his textile empire for almost £2 million.

The "unknown friend" who sent the newspaper cutting probably imagined that Sir James would make a contribution to the fund. However, he not only offered to buy the Parsonage but also contributed £1,500 towards the cost of furnishing it as a museum, and fulfilling the conditions of the Bonnell Bequest which stipulated a fireproof room for the collection.

On August 4, 1928, the Parsonage was handed over to the society as a museum and library. Sir James remarked: "I was born in this parish in the same week in which the unhappy Branwell died; an event followed at intervals of distressing brevity by the deaths of Emily and Anne. Haworth has seen more than a few progressive changes since those far-off times. Her people have moved into closer touch with the wider world and a good many of her children have achieved success in commercial and other pursuits...

"It is to me a somewhat melancholy reflection that I am one of the fast-narrowing circle of Haworth veterans who remember the Parsonage family. I heard Mr Bronte preach, in the pathetic blindness of his old age. Mr Nicholls frequently visited the Schoolhouse as we children ate the mid-day meal in the interval of our elementary studies; while Martha Brown, the faithful servant to whom Mr Bronte gave the money box, the contents of which she was 'to keep ready for a time of need', is still, to me, a well-remembered figure...

"Above all these memorabilia there rises before me the frail, the unforgettable figure of Charlotte Bronte, who more than once stopped to speak a kindly word to the little lad who now stands a patriarch before you. I remember her funeral one Easter-tide and, some six years afterwards, that of her father".

So the Parsonage became the property of the Bronte Society and its rooms were decked out with objects known to the family. Attendance figures help to illustrate the growth of the Bronte cult. In 1927 and 1928, Haworth attracted more visitors than the village had had before. In 1929 numbers began to fall. In 1932, just over 8,000 people paid for admission to the Parsonage. Between 1933 and 1942, there were between 9,000 and 10,000 each year.

The society, faced with rising expenses, was in difficulty again by 1940 when, with 400 members and 9,000 visitors, the income no longer covered current expenditure and modest reserves of cash were being drawn upon. The Council felt anxious that the war would worsen the position. A war-weary population seemed to need the inspiration of the Brontes and visitations rose again to 10,000 for 1941-2-3.

Donald Hopewell, in 1943, pondered on what the society might do at the Parsonage when the war was over. It was hoped to make improvements that would transform it into the "bright, simple place that so impressed Mrs Gaskell". The plate-glass windows would be replaced by dignified square-panel sashes. The glass cases which made the interior "strongly reminiscent of the cheaper kind of shop" would go.

In 1944, attendance figures soared to over 20,000. The figure for 1950, when the Bronte Society had only 542 members, was 49,906. Norman Raistrick, a Haworth man who was appointed custodian of the Parsonage in 1961, was able to report about 82,000 visitors in the first year and a decade later, the figure had risen to 200,000. At Easter alone, some 10,000 people trudged through the famous house.

The attendance peaked in 1974 with an annual figure of 221,000 and the current attendance figure is a more than satisfactory 190,000. The Bronte Society, concerned at the state of the building, and acknowleding that few people wish to tour the building in a crowd, have been attempting to reduce the number of visitors by cutting out its advertising.

The Parsonage is closed from mid-January to February (for spring-cleaning, for conservation work and to instal new exhibitions) but is open on every other day. Video presentations are organised in one of the vaulted cellars, which was converted into a small theatre.

The most important change in recent times has been the introduction of a Bronte bedroom layout. As there was no original bed extant, this was made possible by the commissioning of a modern reproduction of a half-tester bed, based on a drawing by Branwell Bronte. The layout in the Bronte kitchen has been altered to create a more informal and lived-in atmosphere. Mr Bronte's study accords closely with contemporary descriptions of the room.

To some visitors, the Parsonage is Jane Eyre's house. The building appeared in a popular film, *The Railway Children*, and so to many of the youngsters who know little about the Brontes it is "the doctor's house".

10. The "Purple Heather" School
Brontephiles in Bronteland.

...there appears to be no diminution of interest in the Bronte
cult. During the past fortnight, they have come not singly, but
in battalions, so to speak...
Keighley News, in the summer of 1923.

WILLIAM SHARP, writing in *The Pall Mall Magazine* in 1909, mentioned a school of writers and artists whose work extolled the beauty of
the Bronte Moors.

Sharp—like the Purple Heather School—was fond of the long, in-
tricate sentence: "The West Riding moorland and most of the moorlands
of Derbyshire are sombre beyond any other regions of the kind in
England; in stormy and cold weather they may be impressive, but in
the prevailing dull greyness and ever recurring rains they have neither
the spell of 'lovely solitude' nor 'a grave beauty all their own', but often
are simply wide dreary stretches of waste land, without the wildness
and glow and beauty of Exmoor, or of the highlands of Wales and
Cumberland, or of the great moors of Scotland, or even of the heath-
covered rolling heights about Danby, between the York plain and Whit-
by above the sea".

Pause for breath.

Sharp continued: "There are hours in spring, and many days in summer, and sometimes weeks in early autumn, when they are to be seen
in beauty and enjoyed with deep delight by all who love solitude and
great spaces and the breath and freedom of the desert. But ordinarily,
the country is sombre and depressing. . ."

The romantic period came after the fine scholarship of the late Victorian period, when fragments of Charlotte's incomplete novel, *Emma,*
were published and in 1873 came the Haworth Edition of the novels.

Smith, Elder, the publishers of the Haworth Edition, consulted Ellen
Nussey, who perpetuated the idea that the people and places

mentioned in those novels were based on actuality. The illustrator, Wimperis, drew specific places to be found in the Haworth district.

Gradually, through the welter of publicity surrounding Charlotte, the genius of Emily Bronte was recognised; her poems were published and in the 1880s a biography by Mary Robinson commended her work.

The late Victorian period was also notable for "lantern lectures" about the Brontes, when audiences were enchanted by hand-tinted photographs projected on enormous screens.

Among the early lecturers about the Brontes was J Horsfall Turner, of Idle, honorary secretary of the Bronte Society, who confided to a Keighley audience in November, 1894 that he had been in touch with the Rev A B Nicholls, who had promised to supply him with a better picture of himself than the one shown.

Horsfall Turner had begun his lecture by referring to the authors who had at different times enriched the Bronte bibliography, notably Mrs Gaskell, Mr Swinburne, Sir T Wemyss Reid, Dr Peter Bayne, Mr Augustine Birrell and Dr William Wright.

The lecturer was at odds with Mrs Gaskell in her assessment of Haworth and said that the village was not the benighted and outlandish place that she believed it to be, considering that it was well-known as one of the most prominent villages in Yorkshire and Lancashire, and was then, more than now, on one of the main roads or passes to Lancashire and could boast of the visits of men widely known throughout the country. (Doubtless, these included John and Charles Wesley, friends of a former parson, William Grimshaw).

The moors were necessarily bleak and cold in winter, but the lecturer thought that Mrs Gaskell's dark background to her picture of Charlotte Bronte's home was altogether misleading, and that her account of Yorkshire character was equally unwarrantable.

Not only had the Bronte children the practical interest of their father as a cultural literary man, and the inherited literary tastes of their mother, who succumbed to her malady in 1821, but literary efforts were manifesting themselves in and around their village...

One of the writers of the "Purple School", Halliwell Sutcliffe, was the author of moorland romances and is also remembered for his fanciful (but ever-popular) *The Striding Dales*. He was born just outside Bradford but preferred to think of Lee, near Haworth, as his true birthplace, for here he grew up, attending the village school kept by his father. When his father was appointed to a headmastership at Bingley, father and son walked at least once every week over the five miles of moors between Bingley and Haworth.

Sutcliffe was familiar with the lore of the Brontes, of course, and pointed out that, being a mixture of Irish and Cornish, they could not help but write. He thought that they would still have written books about their environment even if they had lived in the East End of London.

Initially, Sutcliffe had to struggle for recognition as a writer. His first book was published in 1893; thereafter he was a prolific author. He tried living in London, but the North called him back and he settled in the Dales, first at Embsay and then (in 1907) at the White Abbey, Linton. When he was not writing, he loved to tend his large rock garden.

He wrote 30 novels, some verse and pageants for Lancaster and Bradford. The article he contributed to the Bronte Society Transactions is so fulsome it makes the modern reader wince. He worked chiefly at night, from about 8-30 pm until the early hours. When he died in 1932 the funeral service took place at Burnsall but his ashes went back to the moors of which he had written so lovingly.

In the *Footsteps of the Brontes*, by Mrs Ellis H Chadwick (1914) contains impressions of the Brontes gained while living in Haworth, followed by residence "on the borders of the *Shirley* country", thence to "within a pleasant walk of Woodhouse Grove".

Mrs Chadwick recounted a tale told by Martha Brown about "Old Mr Bronte going to the kitchen when the specialist said there was no hope of recovery for his daughter and saying: 'I told you, Martha, that there was no sense in Charlotte marrying at all, because she was not strong enough for marriage'."

We read that "Bronte pilgrims may often be seen in the Churchyard, looking over the low wall which separates it from the vicarage garden, but in summer the leafy trees act as a screen to the parsonage. . When the church was pulled down in 1879, Mr. Wade, the incumbent, was very careful that the Bronte grave should not be disturbed, and since the new church was built in 1881, a brass plaque has been fixed over the grave with a simple inscription . . ."

In the 1920s, many airy books romanticised the Brontes and their landscape. Women writers were to the foremost, with Mary Robinson providing *The Life and Eager Death of Emily Bronte* and Elizabeth Southwart a most attractive *Bronte Moors & Villages from Thornton to Haworth*, this latter being notable for the 36 illustrations by T Mackenzie, some reproduced in full colour, the others being drawings, but all highly individualistic.

The authoress wrote of the Bronte pilgrims who had begun to appear in Haworth in 1850 and, by 1895, were in vastly greater numbers, for "ten thousand worshipped at the Bronte shrine. Two-thirds of these chose a day with a cloudless sky—for in such an out-of-the-way place one must not be caught in the rain...

"The greater part of the remaining third of the pilgrims read up, beforehand, all that they could get hold of about the grey tragedy, then went to Haworth seeking what they expected to find—and, as is usually the case in such circumstances, found it...

"Of the writers, however, it is the Yorkshire-born only who have shown no surprise that any good thing can come out of Haworth: and they are accused of the blindness of prejudice, or of keeping up a fiction for loyalty's sake".

This most enjoyable author; this happy pilgrim in Bronteland, sought out the mini-forest of tombstones between the parsonage and Haworth church. We can hear the very tones of that supulchral voice from below, as we read on the tombstone:

> Time was I stood as thou does now
> And viewed the dead as thou dost me:
> Ere long thou'll stand as low as I
> And others stand and look o'er thee.

The humour becomes cynical:

> This world's a city, full of crooked streets,
> Death is the market-place, where all men meet:
> If life was merchandise that men could buy,
> The rich would live, the poor must surely die.

In the "twenties", charabancs raised the dust on unmetalled country roads. The Haworthians became accustomed to seeing them in what had by now become widely known as Bronteland. Haworth was also being proclaimed as "second only to Stratford-on-Avon as a place to be visited by literary enthusiasts".

Jonas Bradley (1859-1943), for many years headmaster of Stanbury school, where he introduced nature study into the school syllabus, resided in the Bronte Country from 1890. He was not a great success as a teacher if success is related to scholarship, but his scholars remembered him with affection.

Jonas knew every inch of the area that was to become known as Bronteland. At one time his star shone as brightly in the Haworth firmament as those of the Brontes themselves. Jonas was a founder member of the Bronte Society and was recognised as an authority on the famous family. His approach to the subject was more human than that of the literary scholar.

As a friend of his wrote on his death: "It was as a genial personality and as a man who could give a vivid, authentic picture of the whole Bronte background that he was sought out by distinguished visitors to Haworth Parsonage".

He and Harold Mitchell, the curator, were fond of leg-pulling. One day Jonas approached Harold and asked him to give a talk to a ramblers' meeting. Harold agreed and in due course he received from Jonas a syllabus noting that he would talk about Trials and Humours of a Curator. There had been a printer's error.

It was given as Carter, not Curator. Harold had a chat with every carter he knew and gave a detailed talk on the ups and down of the carting industry.

In April, 1925, an emissary of *The News Chronicle* met a charabanc party—"plucky Yorkshire folk"—at Haworth, where the main street is "set at an angle of sixty degrees, with its houses and shops jutting out and making all manner of queer geometrical designs". This could not be appreciated on a picture postcard. To see it properly, "you have to climb it, and see. . . a charabanc full of some of the most courageous people in Yorkshire jog painstakingly down".

Both the Church and Bronte Museum were locked. "Not so the *Black Bull*, where Branwell Bronte's triangular chair stands in a corner by the bell pull, which he rang so often to order drinks. You can sit in the chair and order drinks in the same way, but the landlord is ever-ready to show the relic whether you do so or not. And you can write postcards to friends who try to dissuade you from going to Haworth while seated on a great oak settee which came out of the old Church''.

The inter-war years saw the re-discovery of the English countryside by a town-based people whose grandparents had emigrated to the towns looking for work. It was a time of wayside house-shops, where the walker might buy oranges and sweets.

A walker in the Haworth district in the 1920s was to recall the interiors of such little shops—''a glimpse in spotlessly clean parlours of grandfather clocks, capacious bright mahogany chests of drawers and articles of solid furniture such as you do not see in the shops of the city''.

11. That Moaning Wind!
Films, Radio and Television.

Nobody has ever thought of *Wuthering Heights* as an everyday
story of country folk. The wild, mysterious Heathcliff, epitome
of the Byronic hero, is one of the giants of English romantic
literature.
Radio Times, about an adaptation for television, 1978.

Wuthering Heights—real location near Haworth—is being
recreated on Grassington Moor.
Yorkshire Post, September 18, 1991.

THE FIRST of many films based on *Wuthering Heights* was a silent
production made in Haworth in 1920, the director being a Mr Bramble. In the 1930s, the literary aspect of the Brontes flourished and
reached a peak with the publication of a Shakespeare Head edition of
the Life and Letters, which is still the standard text, despite mistakes
and omissions.

Now books were being augmented by wireless productions. An increasing number of radio programmes about the Brontes created further interest in the family and the Haworth neighbourhood. The
20-minute broadcast from Leeds by Jonas Bradley, of Stanbury, in 1934,
proved to be a broadcasting milestone, judged by the number of letters Jonas received.

The letters were rapturous, an example being one from the Sharpe
family of Briarfield: "By gum, it were champion to listen in last neet
to a gradely talk about the Bronte Country". Mr Bateson of Bradford
congratulated Jonas on "a successful score over the Imp known as
MIKE".

J P, of Oxenhope, wrote: "We had all foregathered round the fire
at 10 o'clock in readiness for the announcer calling on you. If you will
allow me to say so, I consider your talk was admirable in every way".

A letter was received from Yorkshire folk who had emigrated to Spain: "We have only had the radio for two weeks and in the first number of the *Radio Times* we were delighted to see your name, that you were to broadcast from Leeds... We got in front of our radio with 'mouths open like throstles' and could hear every word and, knowing all the Haworth district so well, could see it all..."

Before long, films had acquired voices and critical notes were being published. In 1939, Catherine Mabel Edgerley, as part of a memorial tribute by the Bronte Society, considered the classic screen version of *Wuthering Heights* featuring Laurence Olivier and Merle Oberon. Miss Edgerley mentioned the scenery as being wonderfully like Yorkshire, with miles of stone walls and moor and the house, Wuthering Heights, closely resembled "the Withens", though the exterior and the interiors were larger.

She continued: "The Lintons' house perplexes one. Neo-Italian architecture and flunkeys were not found on the moors. The dark atmosphere of morbidity and passion are there and the tragedy of revenge. We see Heathcliff's undefined position in the house of his protector, Mr Earnshaw; how he was bullied and snubbed, how bitterly he resented this and plotted vengeance.

"Laurence Olivier, as Heathcliff, was not detestable enough. Merle Oberon, as Cathy, depicted the wild, primitive passionate girl. As Mrs Linton she was a trifle sophisticated, but she was always charming and irresistible.

"Geraldine Fitzgerald, as Isabella Linton, is the young girl, ready in her innocence to defend anyone badly treated, losing her own heart in doing so. Hugh Williams, as Hindley, is marvellous. His presentation of Hindley as a broken man, sobbing horribly, makes one wince and turn away. Flora Robson, in her two short appearances is a great artist. She is the one comfortable, commonsense, unselfish person. Dressed in black, she suggests a sybil".

Miss Edgerley concluded: "The film is technically perfect; it is a splendid drama".

In the mid-1940s, films and increasing newspaper publicity were reflected in receipts at the Parsonage Museum. In 1944, a film version of *Jane Eyre* made in Hollywood featured Joan Fontaine as Jane and the young Orson Welles as Rochester, with Henry Daniell as Brocklehurst.

A century after the publication of three Bronte novels—Emily's *Wuthering Heights*, Anne's *Agnes Grey* and Charlotte's *Jane Eyre*—the BBC North of England Home Service presented a special programme prepared by Norman Swallow, who introduced it in the *Radio Times* under the title The Elusive Brontes.

Swallow wrote that he had been reading many books about the Brontes but the experience, though interesting in many ways, had taught him surprisingly little about "those strange sisters". It had taught him a good deal about the ways of a biographer and confirmed him in his original belief that the Brontes, despite the mass of research which has been bestowed upon them, are completely elusive.

A broadcast version of *Jane Eyre* by Barbara Couper began an eleven-episode run on radio at the end of February, 1946. The producer was Howard Rose. It was indeed a realistic presentation. Nervous listeners, upset by some of the early scenes at Lowood, were reported to have switched off their radio sets in horror.

H M Raleigh, writing in the Transactions of the Bronte Society, had personal knowledge of more than one occasion when a social engagement was cancelled or postponed because it clashed with an episode in *Jane Eyre*. "I have heard it suggested that the Jane of the radio was thought too sprightly and vivacious, but I doubt if that opinion is widely shared, and to me Belle Chrystall, with her calm, sweetly modulated tones, stirred only occasionally by gusts of passionate emotion, *was* Jane as I had always imagined her, while the gruff timbre of Reginald Tate's voice carried just that 'tone of command' which Rochester, at an early interview with his child's governess, asked her to excuse".

In the same issue of Transactions was a note about a "vulgar distortion" by Hollywood of the life of the Brontes. At the time of writing, it had been seen in New York but had not yet been screened in Britain.

A critic who witnessed a trade show in this country wrote: "Emily (played by Ida Lupino) is passionately in love with the Reverend A B Nicholls (Paul Henreid), a 'Boyeresque' clergyman, but he is in love with Charlotte (Olivia de Havilland), and so, out of devotion to her sister, Emily leaves the way clear for the lovers by going into a decline, while the celestial choir bursts into song and the ghostly 'Dark Horseman' from Wuthering Heights puts in an appearance".

Wrote the *New York Post*: "The names of places and people are correct. Some of the dates and events are not too far off; but the rest is a horrible example of what Hollywood can do to make a bad name for itself in the handling of historic personages whose lives should be treated with high regard for the truth as far as it is known...They have got just enough of the Brontes' lives into the picture to make it false and distorted. To those who would not know a Bronte from a blondie any way, the picture is not bad as a genteel costume romance".

Cyril Dunn kept a watching brief for the Bronte Society on March 7, 1948, when *Wuthering Heights* was given its first television broadcast from a studio in Alexandra Palace. "Within this Palace full of gadgets, Miss Bronte was most properly received. The transformation of her work into its latest medium was quite evidently treated as an occasion".

This version was "reduced to uninterrupted dialogue because, one imagines, television cannot exploit a pause". The action was confined to one or two status corners of the farmhouse. "There were one or two glances into the rural district beyond the windows, and once Heathcliff stood by the open door while a wind-machine tore at his ensemble, but these resources were not rewarding.

"Hemmed in by arc-lamps and cameras of restricted mobility, the performance seemed to be taking place on top of an occasional table, with the players constantly restrained by the fear that Bronte passion too freely expressed would entangle them in the studio's fittings".

Mr Keiron Moore (Heathcliff) was "struck smartly on the head by an arc-lamp during rehearsal and the recollection of this incident seemed, reasonably enough, to cramp his style...The production was justified, in the artistic sense, primarily by the opportunity it gave to Miss Katharine Blake, the young South African with the long, dark hair, who played Catherine Earnshaw. She was virtually alone in creating an absolute illusion, in making one forget the gadgets".

It might be called "a brave effort". Mr Dunn heard only one serious attempt to speak the Yorkshire tongue "and this, I regret to say, was in the 'oop for't Coop' tradition of the London stage".

James R Gregson. West Riding born and bred, brought a much more authentic atmosphere to his three-episode dramatisation of *Wuthering Heights*, broadcast from Leeds in the autumn of 1947. He devised each episode—The Foundling, The Usurper, The Master—to cover a different phase of Heathcliff's life and to be a dramatic entity.

By February, 1956, *Jane Eyre* had been adapted for the theatre, filmed and transmitted as a radio serial and had begun a six week's run as a television serial.

Wuthering Heights, adapted for the theatre by Brian Tyler in 1964, disappointed Peter Holdsworth, theatre critic of the *Telegraph and Argus*, who wrote: "It would not be honest to pretend it is an entire success . . . It strikes a jarring, melodramatic note where it should be Wagnerian. It gives us cardboard instead of millstone grit. It gives us hysteria instead of demonic fury. In other words, it gives us little of that Emily who was said to be in love with the Absolute".

In 1970, the American film-makers returned to the West Riding to "shoot" scenes for a new version of *Wuthering Heights*. They were not too happy about doing this at Haworth and found other places where the Victorian atmosphere lingered. One of the producers remarked: "We scoured for sites there (Haworth), but always there was some difficulty which would have marred the picture. It's a shame . . . "

It was a worthy film, starring Timothy Dalton and Anna Calder-Marshall, but filming Bronte works tends to be a high-risk operation; this production—like two others before it—flopped at the box office.

Brontemania raged in 1973 and the estimated number of tourists at Haworth was well over one million. Many were lured by the two television series on the Brontes that ran simultaneously.

It was no longer necessary to do all the filming at Haworth. The Yorkshire Television series of 1973 made use of the exterior of the Parsonage but mocked-up some of the interiors at their Kirkstall Road studios in Leeds. Filming in the main street took place in the early morning, and the yellow lines which discourage parking were temporarily covered with peat moss.

It was an impressive series, though Nina Hibbin, writing in *November in Yorkshire*—admittedly when the series was only half over—thought that by weighing his scripts fairly heavily with commentary, Christopher Fry had supposedly adopted the documentary reconstruction approach. Yet considering the length of the episodes, there was, added Nina, surprisingly little narrative detail. "His linquistic subtleties are elegant but uneconomical in a medium which is fundamentally visual".

In the autumn of 1978, the British Tourist Authority launched a film, *The Yorkshire of the Bronte Sisters*, which would, over the following four years, be seen by an estimated 300 million overseas viewers. A writer in the *Keighley News*—possibly Bill Black, the Editor, a Brontephile—shuddered at the thought.

In this film, Haworth was highly romanticised. The place was depicted as "a quaint village idyllically positioned amidst the rolling sun-drenched moors. Nowhere was to be seen the true Haworth of the Bronte sisters—the bleak village clinging tenaciously to the windswept Pennines. For nine months of the year, and that is being generous, the place battles against the elements, those same harsh elements whistling off the moors that 200 years ago contributed tragically to the premature deaths of those three brilliant sisters".

A Bronte production of 1974 was the world premiere by the Royal Ballet of Ronald Hynd's *Charlotte Bronte*; it was the Haworth story seen through her eyes, staged at the Bradford Alhambra. Dramatic highlights included the love affair between Branwell and Mrs Robinson (!) and a few death scenes. Hynd, thrilled by the actual setting, said that the moors had given the ballet an instant lyrical starting point.

The producers of radio, film and television return again and again to the Bronte theme. Some of the offerings are individualistic, an example being a BBC documentary by A N Wilson, part of a series entitled *Eminent Victorians*. Others are put together on a shoe-string, for insertion into one of the regular topical programmes, a prime example of this being a most appealing mini-series featuring Anna Massey with Ian Dewhirst, who at that time was the Reference Librarian at Keighley.

And so to this present day. In August, 1991, *The Daily Mail* reported: "The decision to cast a French actress as female lead in a new film version of *Wuthering Heights* is provoking anger and derision in the British movie industry". Juliette Binoche, who was described by the newspaper as "sultry", had been given the role of Cathy Earnshaw in a £10m production.

A reference was made by a critic to the inappropriate nature of a "lisping French accent". The newspaper reported that Juliette was in London having dialect coaching. In October, that same newspaper mentioned the start of filming "in the windswept Yorkshire Dales".

What of the star? She was "an alluring blend of Gallic sexuality and childlike innocence". Insiders on the set believed she did have the perfect qualities to play "Heathcliff's passionate and petulant lover". The producer, Mary Selway, was reported to have said of Juliette Binoche: "She absolutely is Cathy. She has her spirit and her passion". Heathcliff would be played by a Shakespearean actor, Ralph Fiennes. The singer Sinead O'Connor had the part of a silent Emily Bronte.

That autumn, it was to Yarnbury near Grassington—not Haworth — that the filmsters went for mooredge scenes in this expensive re-make of the old story. In September, a Yorkshire newspaper published a photograph of sheep farmer Robert Stockdale guiding his flock along a lane near a five-storey Wuthering Heights mansion. Soon, large numbers of people converged where a team of 12 engineers from Shepperton Studios in London were building what was said to be a replica of Heathcliff's home.

Although the house stood in a limestone area it was close to a geological "fault" and over the wall lay an impressive tract of millstone grit, lagged with peat and thatched with heather. A wind that wuthered on most days of the week made the imported wind-machine redundant.

The mock-up of the facade of Wuthering Heights may have suited the film-makers but it was far too pretentious to be of the Pennines. The media thrives on exaggeration and this building served its purpose well, being fanciful, romantic and with a Disneyish flavour.

I parked my swaying car near some ash trees that were flailing their branches as the wind strengthened into a westerly gale. The track lay near a dispersal point for materials used to create the illusion of ancient, solid masonry (rap a stone with your knuckle and a hollow sound might be heard). This masonry had been delivered in thick grey rolls.

Solid-looking gateposts stood where none had existed a few days before. Standing on tiptoe, I looked over the wall to take in the form and character of Wuthering Heights. Jane Sellars, Director of the Bronte Society, interviewed by *The Daily Mail* about this construction, said: "I think Wuthering Heights should be a low-lying, stone farmhouse with other buildings added on. It would certainly not be tall or grand".

Also in view were bundles of reeds and a four-wheeled cart. The gale tore at newly-introduced trees and shrubs, displacing some of the vegetation and teasing a large thorn tree. Once again, I was impressed by the skill of film-makers in creating illusions. The ponderous building was no more than a facade, held upright by a mass of scaffolding.

Hearing of the transformation of a moor-edge barn into a chapel, I passed the forlorn wind-machine and took a track normally followed by students of lead-mining in an area where a number of kings' ransoms in lead had been hacked from the veins and smelted on site.

In a quiet little valley beyond the remains of the smelt mill is a field barn—only it had now been transformed into a country church. The barn provided the body of a structure which had now sprouted a tower and porch. This modern game of make-believe extended to an adjacent croft where a graveyard had appeared overnight.

The inscribed stones looked substantial and ancient, yet each was of light construction with a wooden flange for stability. The moorland sheep were using some of them as "scratting posts".

The Bronte home at Thornton.

12. Marketing the Brontes
The Tourist Industry

Go shopping in Haworth's cobbled Main Street, where Branwell
used to buy opium...And then walk it all off on the famous
Bronte moors, which inspired those classic novels.
Summertime, a free-sheet published at Keighley (1991).

HAWORTH'S period of greatest change as a literary shrine followed
the 1939-45 war. The village already had a Bronte Fish and Chip Shop,
a Bronte Cinema and a Bronte Bus Service. Now the Bronte name was
much more widely used.

The clearance of what someone referred to as "a hotch-potch of
snickets and allotments" at the lower end was done with the laudable
idea of creating a traffic by-pass to reduce the flow of vehicles over
the stone setts. A consequence was that old Haworth lost a sense of
mystery. It had previously been an adventure to climb the hill, through
a gritstone gorge.

On the 150th anniversary of the birth of Charlotte, which fell in April
1966, a writer in the *Halifax Evening Courier and Guardian* reported
that "ballooning Bronte business and status as a 'literary shrine' have
given their drab moorland village little else but publicity and traffic
jams. Money spent by the thousands of visitors all seems to go to a few
shops and cafes". The Parsonage Museum had 1,800 "customers"—
paying 2s each—on Easter Monday alone.

A local publican told the reporter that Haworth folk do not understand "all this Bronte fuss" and were bored, amused or irritated by it.
They felt to be living in a place that existed just for other people. They
were having to keep up appearances—Victorian appearances—so that
the place would have an "unspoiled" look.

In that anniversary year, Mrs Joanna Hutton was curator of a Bronte
Parsonage Museum which was visited by almost 68,000 people, a considerable number being from America and Japan. The Bronte Society,

which then had a membership of 1,200, observed Charlotte's birthday by laying wreaths at Poets' Corner in Westminster Abbey and at Haworth Church, which then was needing another £2,000 to undertake the repair of the organ. Someone visiting the Parsonage had, despite its elaborate system of burglar alarms, stolen old Mr Bronte's watch and the pistol he discharged from the window every morning.

Haworth was going through a messy period. The newspaper writer mentioned a deeply-rutted coach park, the unmade streets, empty houses and a general untidiness. Today it is a tidy, touristy place, with a friendly atmosphere. The staff at the information centre play a key role in dispensing good advice and cheap or free publications. In the many little shops, images of the Brontes appear on tea-towels, notepaper and the covers of publications. Books about the Brontes and the Bronte Country have proliferated.

In murky November, a thousand lights stained the mist as Haworth prepared itself for an Old Tyme Christmas, complete with Bronte costumes, Christmas lights, brass bands, harmony singers, jazz band, town crier, Santa Claus and Mother Christmas. These attractions were outlined on a leaflet issued by the Bradford Metropolitan Countryside Service, who urged readers to "enjoy a wonderful Christmas in Haworth: Home of the Brontes". On the attendant map—as on some of the signposts—Withens had become Withins.

A Haworthian commended the torchlight procession as "summat special", for after processing up Main Street to the church the annual carol service took place.

In a cafe where I had simple Yorkshire fare—tea, biscuit and scone—I let my eyes range along the products with Bronte pictures, including Yorkshire Biscuits, the wrapping featuring a colour photograph of the Parsonage.

In the autumn of 1991, the British Wool Marketing Board took Cathy and Heathcliff to Tokyo, more precisely to the Mitsukoshi store, where a British Fair was being held. The store requested that the short presentation should include drama, music and dance and be based on *Wuthering Heights*. The Arbeau Dancers played the parts of the Brontes and also demonstrated some of the popular dances of the period. Ann Lloyd was Cathy and a local amateur actor, Paul Henly, played the part of Heathcliff.

In the end it is to the moors we go for the true Bronte spirit and for an explanation of the Bronte cult. The moorland endures as a special sort of Bronte landscape.

These Bronte moors are small in size as compared with those of the High Dale Country or the North York Moors. Emily Bronte's moors— the moors of her mind —are vast and elemental. Emily is revealed as the greatest of the Bronte writers and *Wuthering Heights* is the book that sustains the Bronte interest.

My latest visit was in late summer, as the Bronte heather bloomed and Bronte rowans stood with armsful of tinted leaves and vermilion berries. At the moor-edge I parked my car on newly-spread limestone chippings which had brought some geological confusion to an area where gritstone is the dominant rock. Haworth itself was incapable of accepting another parked car.

This Penistone Hill parking and picnic area offered space and good views. One of the last of the summer curlews drifted by, giving the familiar bubbling call. The Bronte breeze played games with an empty cola tin.

For some, the car park was a home from home. I watched a middle-aged couple, whose penetration of Bronteland would be no more than 50 yards, arrange collapsible chairs and a table. Their needs were simple: fresh air and moorland views. While the man sat and stared, his wife took from the boot of the car the plastic containers holding afternoon tea.

Children fantasised about the American Badlands as they scrambled on the gritstone boulders of the old quarries and scanned the clear horizons. Visitors, with the patience of coolies in a paddy field, collected bilberries. A coach party, obsessed with toilets and tea, was heading back towards Haworth.

I joined the trickle of Bronte fans on a pilgrimage to Top Withens, the position of which was indicated by a few trees breaking a distant horizon. At first, the track was fringed by willow herb, the rose-purple flowers of which prepared me for the heather moor, which now, in late summer, wore its cloak of imperial purple. The bell heather had flowered and withered; the ling sported flowers which would soon be issuing clouds of pollen like fine white dust.

I took a diagonal route to cross a farm track, approaching the Bronte

Waterfall from above. The clough was rimmed with grouse butts. I did not hear a single grouse, which is not surprising on a hot afternoon in summer. I walked into a cloud of flies and winged beetles, passing under the steely gaze of moorland yows, all but one clipped, and watched huge lambs drain the last of the milk from their weary mothers.

The Bronte Falls were just a trickle. One cascade led into a peat-brown pool which had white froth upon it and looked for all the world like ale. No one was sitting in the Bronte Chair—the L-shaped rock with "C. Bronte" inscribed on the back—but other boulders were in use. A Japanese family was reading the Japanese sub-titles on a signpost.

The Bronte Bridge had been repaired after being swept away by a flash flood in the spring of 1989. With its carefully positioned flagstones, it looked far too neat. Large, rough slabs would have been more fitting.

I went up the hillside and along the well-beaten path leading in easy stages to Top Withens. The Bronte wind did not so much "wuther" as caress a landscape dried by sun and wind. I was overtaken by two young men with dogs on leads and by two young women who were talking so loudly they were involving passers-by in some dreary talk about last night's rave-up. A young Japanese man with a grave look on his face held a volume (presumably a Bronte novel) clasped in one hand.

I passed another signpost with Japanese sub-titles, this one having, after a few weeks, lost the inset discs which provide the paths with colour coding. At Top Withens I once again shuddered at the lack of sensitivity shown by those who arrested the collapse of the buildings by levelling them off. The impression, from the approach path, is of some grand mausoleum. It must be the saddest-looking ruin in England.

Yet I exulted in the sights and sounds and the many Bronte associations. There must have been Life Before the Brontes—but it cannot have amounted to much!

Some Books About the Brontes

Gaskell, EC, *Life of Charlotte Bronte* 3 Vols (Smith, Elder, 1857)

Lane, M, *The Bronte Story: A Reconsideration of Mrs Gaskell's Life of Charlotte Bronte* (Heinemann, 1953)

Lock, J and Dixon, W T, *A Man of Sorrow: The Life, Letters and Times of the Rev. Patrick Bronte* (Nelson, 1965)

Kellett, J, *Haworth Parsonage: The Home of the Brontes* (The Bronte Society, Haworth, 1977)

Lloyd Evans, G & B, *Everyman's Companion to the Brontes* (Dent, 1982)

Transactions of the Bronte Society, annually since 1895 (The Bronte Society)